PEOPLE'S OF ROMAN BRITAIN

General Editor: Keith Branigan
Professor of Prehistory and Archaeology
University of Sheffield

The Carvetii

NICHOLAS HIGHAM

Staff Tutor in History

and

BARRI JONES

Professor of Archaeology,
Univeristy of Manchester

ALAN SUTTON

First published in the United Kingdom in 1985 by
Alan Sutton Publishing Ltd · Phoenix Mill · Far Thrupp
Stroud · Gloucestershire

Reprinted 1991

First published in the United States of America in 1991 by
Alan Sutton Publishing Inc · Wolfeboro Falls · NH 03896–0848

British Library Cataloguing in Publication Data

Higham, Nick
   The Carvetti. – (Peoples of Roman Britain).
   1. Cumbria (England), history, to 410
   I. Title   II. Jones, Barri   III. Series
   936.27804

   ISBN 0-86299-088-2

Library of Congress Cataloging in Publication Data applied for

Typesetting and origination by
Alan Sutton Publishing Limited.
Printed in Great Britain by
The Bath Press, Bath, Avon.

Contents

To
Our Cumbrian Friends

Acknowledgements

While the aim of this book is that of its companions in the series, namely the archaeological survey of a cantonal region, the gestation of this survey is somewhat different. It has been produced largely as a result of an active and continuing programme of aerial photography, fieldwork and excavation by the authors. Indeed, the desirability of checking new air photographic evidence on the ground by excavation has delayed the production of this book, which in places would otherwise have been a repetition of very limited and often dated evidence, particularly on the agricultural economy. By presenting substantially new material throughout the authors hope to offer a thorough reassessment of an area of great archaeological richness for which any archaeological synthesis on the larger scale has so far been lacking.

As a result the acknowledgements of support, both financial and otherwise, are more numerous than usual. Direct funding for part of the projects incorporated in this book was derived from the Society of Antiquaries of London, the British Academy, the Mouswald Trust, the BBC Chronicle Unit, the Countryside Commission, the Department of the Environment Inspectorate for Ancient Monuments, the Cumberland and Westmorland Antiquarian and Archaeological Society and the R.J. Kiln Trust. Certain other aspects were funded by the University of Manchester and its Department of Extra Mural Studies, but much of the fieldwork and in particular, the aerial photography, was paid for by the authors. The programme of aerial photography would not have been possible without the support and encouragement of Brian and Anne Berry, Ian and Dorothy Bewley, and their son Robert.

Gordon and Mary Dixon were a constant source of help, and work on the Solway coast was particularly assisted by Mr W. Johnston and the late Mr T. Jones, History Master and Headmaster respectively at Silloth Secondary School, the pupils of which provided considerable help in 1977 and 1978. Mr Noel Dyas of Bowness provided valuable information on the Solway estuary. Mrs Sheila Smart organised much local support in the Penrith area along with Mr S. Urquhart and Mr M. Huffthwaite, and Mr and Mrs Mary Messenger did the same in the Wigtown area. At Kirkby Stephen much help and advice was provided by Mr and Mrs Dargue of Smardale, and Messrs, J. Relph, A. Swailes and R. Downing. The help from Burgh-by-Sands deserves a special thank you, notably to Mr and Mrs G. Reid, and the Rev. and Mrs J. Strong. A special debt of thanks is owed to farmers who gave permission for excavations to take place on their land, notably Mr and Mrs Campbell Reid of Burgh-by-Sands, Mr and Mrs L. Hodson of Easton, Mr and Mrs R. Wills of Fingland Rigg and Mrs Martin of Monkhill. The excavation of the Penrith Farm took place by courtesy of Mr W. Threlfield, that of Dobcross thanks to Mr R. Holliday, that at Castle Hill, Waitby, thanks to Mr R. Hewitson, and at Bothel to Mr Pallister.

Academic advice is gratefully acknowledged to a number of sources: Professor A.C. Thomas, Mr T. Clare, Mr M. McCarthy whose Carlisle Unit also helped complete work at Burgh-by-Sands in 1978, Mr A.E. Truckell, Mr L. Masters, Mr G. Jobey, Professor R. Cramp, Mr C.M. Daniels, Mr J.P. Gillam and Professor E. and Mr R. Birley, as well as Professors J.K. St Joseph, J.J. Wilkes and J.C. Mann, Miss D. Charlesworth, Miss C. Fell, and Dr B. Matthews of the Soils Survey. In particular Prof. A.R. Birley kindly read the final draft of this book to its considerable improvement.

The scheme would not have been brought near completion without the help of a number of former students, postgraduates and others, who have consistently helped, under all weather conditions, over the last few years, particularly Mr P. Bennett, Mr D. Evans, Mr D. Mattingly, Mr P. James, Mr J.H. Allen, Mr R. Wallace, Mr P. Reynolds, Mr J.D. Blackburn, Mr J. Manley, Mr P. Hudson, Mr J. Triscott, Mr N. Warr, Mr A Tinsley, J. and R. Marshall, J. Moss, Miss A.

Goodier and Miss S. Worthington.

The production of several of the illustrations stems from the work of Dr P. Holder, Mr D. Powlesland, Mrs J. Laughton and in particular, Miss C. Turnock of the Department of Archaeology, Manchester University, where the organisation of the annual programme of work was largely carried out by Mrs Angela Roden, Miss Jane Carwford, Miss Linda Whitaker, Mrs Jenny McCleery, Mrs Sylvia Hazelhurst and, in particular, Mr Keith Maude. To these and others too numerous to mention the authors extend their most sincere thanks.

List of Illustrations

*Line drawings by Jennifer Gill, Nicholas Higham
and Barri Jones*

1

Tribal Territory and the
Pre-Roman Iron Age

The Cumbrian and Scottish territory of the tribe that we know as the Carvetii is one of the most mountainous areas south of the Forth-Clyde isthmus. The expanses of habitable terrain are limited to the coastal plains of the northern and western territory in Cumberland, and in coastal south-west Scotland, and the valleys of the rivers draining into the Solway basin – in particular the Eden and its several tributaries, the Annan, the Nith and the Irthing (Fig. 1). These tracts of relatively low lying terrain contain limited areas of Grade 2 agricultural land,[1] in particular concentrated in the Central Eden valley around Penrith, and in the Cumberland Plain near Carlisle and Wigton. The best soils are to be found on a sandstone substrate, but workable loams are found elsewhere on the widespread glacial drift, sands and clays of the valleys. There are marked exceptions to this even in the low lying valley floors: expanses of heavy, wet clay are typical of many of the areas which in the medieval period were given over to forest, typified by the great royal forest of Inglewood. The other low-lying uninhabitable areas are peat deposits on mudstones and clay, present on both sides of the Solway estuary and in the Debateable Lands north and east of Carlisle. The potential for settlement in these areas is restricted to the eskers of sand and gravel which are a common feature particularly in northern Cumberland, west of the Wampool.

These low lying areas are bordered by substantial areas of mountainous terrain. One type of high ground that has attracted widespread settlement, is the limestone uplands that fringe the valleys of the Eden and its tributaries, and of the Lune, where good drainage and local high alkilinity compen-

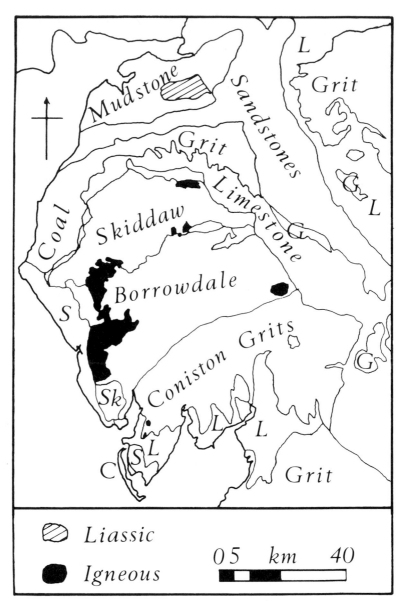

Fig. 1   The geology of the territory of the Carvetti

sate for the acidic tendencies of rainfall often far in excess of 40" (98 cm.). The fact that these limestone fells have seen little intensive land use since the Roman period has allowed a high level of site survival to have occurred, and has caused a concentration of attention on these areas to the detriment of others where evidence has been less obvious.

Other areas of high ground are dominated by older rocks – Ordovican, Cambrian and Silurian – which make up most of the central lakeland massif, and gritstones which comprise the high Pennines. Much of these areas is too high for early settlement and land-use – with exceptions, of course, such as the hill-fort on Carrock Fell. However, the lower slopes of these terrains often provide evidence of marginal land-use – for example, in the cairn fields of the west Cumberland coast, as low as 200–250m above O.D., and even the extensive field-systems as on Aughertree Fell to the south of Wigton. To some extent it seems possible to argue for environmental deterioration accounting for abandonment to extensive, poor pasture on some of these terrains.

Mountains form a natural frontier to the territory – the Pennines to the east, the Cumbrian Massif to the west and south, and the Southern Scottish Uplands to the north. Certainly these are the boundaries that make sense from a topographical viewpoint, defining a territory stretching from the Rhinns of Galloway to the Upper Irthing Valley, and from the Upper Annan to Shap, Tebay or Kirkby Lonsdale to the south.

Pre-Roman Settlement in the North-West

The area now known to have been inhabited by the Carvetii is one that has seen little modern archaeological research. With the exception of a series of excavations at the Mesolithic sites at Eskmeals, the pre-Roman community has been badly neglected. In practise, it is fair to say that archaeology has been dominated by the investigation of the Roman military sites that are particularly common there, to the detriment of all other studies. To date, there has not been excavated a single site that has provided unequivocal evidence of occupation in the pre-Roman iron age, although a handful of cases have been put forward. The little we can surmise about the area in the late prehistoric period is derived from pollen diagrams, small scale and often early excavations, fieldwork, analogy with other areas, and a limited amount of historical information relating directly to the Conquest.

Pollen analysis from widespread lakes and bogs has revealed a process of deforestation by man stretching back almost 4,000 years before Christ. By the end of the first millennium b.c., some of the better drained areas of southern Lakeland and of the coastal and riverine plain of the Solway and Eden had been permanently cleared, along with much of the uplands of the southern half of the lakeland massif.[2] Elsewhere, small-scale and temporary clearances had occurred, but there is little sign of full-scale forest clearance before the Roman era.

That a bronze age population utilised this area can be shown by the presence of artifactual evidence (Fig. 2). The only reasonably prolific finds have been pottery and metalwork, in both cases scattered across the lowland areas, but with a definite concentration in the Central Eden valley around Penrith and the Eamont, and to a lesser extent in the Morecambe lowlands of Furness and Cartmel.[3] The presence of the only two substantial henge monuments in North West England on the Eamont River – and the records of a further possible example destroyed in the nineteenth century[4] – suggests some real nucleation of an organised society in the second millennium with a centre of at least spiritual, and probably also socio-political, significance in the Eden-Eamont basin where the best farming land in the territory is to be found. The settlement sites that would lend some credibility to this hypothesis have not been identified, but nor has any attempt been made to find them.

The largest and best known candidate for the late prehistoric tribal centre is the stone built hill-fort on the top of Carrock Fell, lying on the first range of hills above the valleys of the Eden and Petteril. Collingwood[5] argued that this site showed evidence of intentional slighting and suggested that it represented the stronghold of the local Brigantian resistance to Roman conquest and suffered demolition as a result. In practice, the site is unlikely to have been so important, and

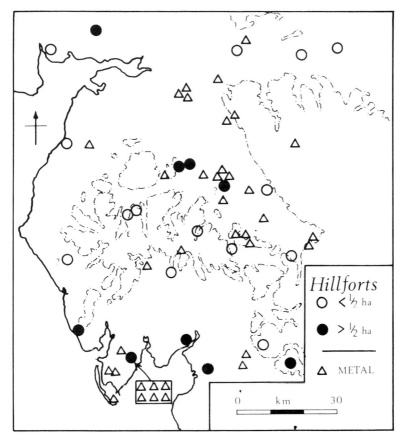

Fig. 2   Cumbria in Later Prehistory

(? Contours shown at *1000 ft. AOD*)

need not have been in use so late. Sited on terrain above 300m, there is no evidence of internal structures or traces of permanent population. The fort would be more likely to relate to a scattered, and perhaps transhumant population, in the Eden Valley, in the central Lakeland area (via the Troutbeck-Keswick route) and on the north Cumberland plain. North of the Solway, several substantial late prehistoric forts are known, for example at Burnswark and Wardlaw, but south of the estuary alternative sites are, on the whole, small multival-

late or univallate settlements which upon excavation turn out
to be occupied in the Roman period (e.g. Waitby Castle).
Only two sites are likely candidates. At Dobcross Hall,
Dalston, a double-ditched enclosure, over 7 acres (3 ha.) in
area, is probably of two periods.[6] The defensive nature of the
outer ditch and the scarp top site indicate a pre-Roman date,
and given the evidence of a radiating ditch system it may have
been an important pastoralist centre. Within it, a small,
central enclosure was occupied in the Roman period (Fig. 3).

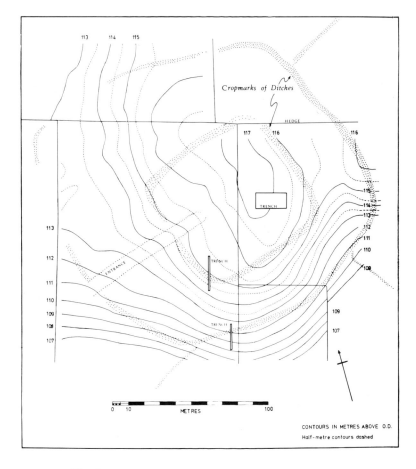

Fig. 3   A two-period site at Dobcross Hall, Dalston

The second, and by far the most likely, is the previously unrecorded site at Clifton Dykes, just south of Brougham, where a substantial earthwork enclosing at least 7 acres (3 ha.) has only been demolished by agricultural activity in the last two decades. Clifton Dykes has to be preferred on the grounds of its better strategic situation, and its location in the centre of the best agricultural land, but to date Clifton Dykes has provided no evidence of the date of occupation. In the south and west, the Skelmore Heads hill fort clearly has bronze age connections, and a newly discovered, bivallate fort near Millom probably served a similar function.

In practice, there is only negligible evidence for an iron age culture in the territory prior to the Roman conquest. It has been argued that rural settlement sites at Wolsty and Crosby Ravensworth[7] date from this period, but the evidence is unconvincing and the pollen record implies that little settled agriculture was taking place. Settlement sites of bronze age type are more easily located. Considerable cairn fields, in some cases associated with hut circles and enclosures are common on marginal terrains, particularly on the western and southern slopes of the central mountain range. In many ways the most instructive of these is that at Shap Wells, north of Tebay on the Eden-Lune watershed.[8] A widespread scatter of cairns is in this case associated with collapsed stone walls and both unenclosed and enclosed hut sites, near a defensive hilltop enclosure at Shap Wells Hotel, with a 'banjo' style entranceway and associated hut circles and enclosures. The system appears to have been designed for at least limited agricultural exploitation, with surface stone being removed to form cairns and boundary walls. Even so, the marginal terrain and the funnel-shaped entrances to the defensive hilltop enclosure suggest that this was superseded by a broadly animal-based economy centred on a small defensive nucleus. Similar evidence comes from the unenclosed hut circles and associated stonewalls and cairns at Blue Quarry, also in Shap parish. However, evidence of land enclosure and cultivation prior to the erection of military installations early in the second century comes from Tarraby Lane, near Carlisle[9] and from Carrawburgh.

There would at first sight appear to be considerable differences between an exploitation complex of the Shap Wells type and the scatter of farm sites that emerge as the basic pattern of settlement in the Roman period. However, we should beware of arguing for any profound change in the pattern of rural society being due solely to the Roman conquest. The stone hut circles and their associated features fit most easily into a bronze age context. While it is arguable that a bronze age culture was still dominant in the area at the end of the first century A.D., this is by no means proven. What is worth noting is the wide incidence of settlement and land-use evidence of 'native' type (as opposed to Roman or Continental) present in the area in the second century A.D.

The settlement sites of the first half of the Roman period, with their round huts and enclosures, are morphologically indistinguishable from the range of 'native' traditions of rural settlement anywhere in England from Northumberland to Wessex, dated to the second half of the first millennium B.C. Similarly, the standard types of land enclosure – the drystone wall, the earth 'dyke' and small ditched or walled fields – to be found in this area are derived from cultural origins of 'native' and not Roman source, ultimately from bronze age cultures already identified in detail elsewhere in the province. Unless we should argue for the substantial movement of a British population into this area at the end of the first century A.D., the available evidence is best explained by the presence of a substantial and widespread population of bronze age origins utilising techniques common to the rural population over wide areas of Britain (and areas on the Continent), but without any (or any substantial quantity of) pottery in use. Such an argument would at least fit in best with the most likely hypotheses concerning the Roman conquest of northern Brigantia, wherein the great encampment or fort at Stanwick Pass would seem to. be associated with a defence of the Stainmore Pass, and would thereby prevent penetration of the Eden-Solway area from the east. Indeed it is possible, as Tacitus distinguishes the *regnum*, or kingdom, of *Cartimandua*, queen of the Brigantes, from that of her first husband, *Venutius*, that he was particularly associated with the Carvetian area, or further north.

The identification of the civitas

The Brigantes, and who they were, present one of the perennial problems of Roman Britain. However specific the term may have been in scope, it is clear several Roman writers used the name generically to cover the natives of North Britain.[10]

We are on firmer ground in identifying some of the sub-tribes or septs that made up the overall confederacy. The Parisi of Humberside are perhaps the most obvious example,[11] with distinctive grave types recognisable in their area. Much of their history in the conquest period would be more intelligible if it were possible to assume that Cartimandua, the pre-Roman queen had particularly strong links with this tribal sub-grouping.[12] Other septs are also known; the Setantii appear to have lived in the area of central Lancashire and the Fylde. In the north-west it is now also possible to identify the tribe, or sub-tribe, known as the Carvetii. A few years ago this could not have been done with any certainty. An inscription from Old Penrith[13] referred to a certain Flavius Martius who was described as being a *senator* in either the cohort or canton of the Carvetii. Either interpretation was possible, since the rank of *senator* is attested in the late Roman army, but the issue was settled in 1964 when a fresh milestone was located at Brougham.[14] The abbreviation *R.P.C. Car* at the end of the inscription relates without doubt to *respublica civitatis Car(vetiorum)* in the manner of an inscription attested amongst the Silures.[15]

The combination of these two inscriptions allows us to infer the existence of the *civitas Carvetiorum*, or canton of the Carvetii, and the existence of its own council or governing body. Fortunately the proximity of the two findspots also suggests that the Eden valley was the heartland of the area concerned. Indeed one might argue further. While in the main period with which we are concerned Carlisle was clearly the most important military and civilian centre, this was not necessarily always the case. The communication crossroads of the area then, as it still is today, lay at Penrith where four major natural routeways converge. There, on the south side of Eamont Bridge, as mentioned above, are two visible, and one destroyed, henge monuments which attest the importance of the area to earlier prehistoric peoples as a hosting place. Furthermore, the size of the little-known settlement site of Clifton Dyke (above p. 7) places it in a different class from any other native site in the area with the possible exceptions of Dobcross Hall and Bishop's Dyke near Dalston (if indeed the latter is not medieval in date). Although now invisible at ground level Clifton Dykes can be seen from aerial photography to have covered an area of over 7 acres (3 ha.) and its size and position overlooking the best grade land in the whole Eden valley[16] make it the logical candidate for the *caput Carvetiorum*. It might also be a factor in the siting of *Brocavum*, the Roman fort at Brougham, a kilometre to the north at the crossing of the Eamont. One of the most intriguing features at Brougham (discussed more fully on p. 64) is the way in which it has yielded more instances of dedications to the god Belatucadrus than any other site (Fig. 4). The cult was

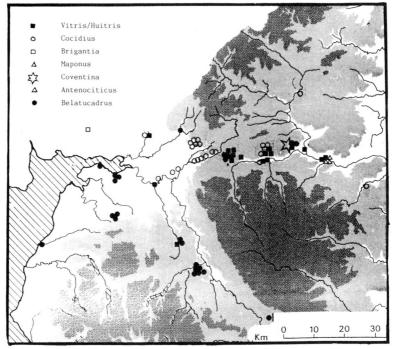

Fig. 4 Romano-Celtic dedications in the territory of the Carvetti

confined to Cumbria and the western edge of Northumberland and seven of its twenty known dedications are to be found at Brougham,[17] a site that has seen little excavation[18] and none at all within the fort interior. The point to emphasise is that Belatucadrus was evidently worshipped as a martial deity conflated only with Mars as opposed to other more pacific deities in the Roman period. The occurrence of his epigraphically attested dedications coincides closely with the distribution of representations of the horned god in the North-West and the combination of two dedications found in proximity to a horned deity at Burgh-by-Sands makes the conflation highly likely, if not certain.[19]

The Brougham area, therefore, with its proximity to the Eamont Bridge henges (which like the Clochmabenstane megaliths continued to mark a meeting place into the medieval period) and the presumed pre-Roman tribal capital at Clifton Dykes, emerges as the leading candidate for the location of the cult centre of Belatucadrus the horned god of the Brigantes, a deity moreover known only for his warlike qualities. These factors would readily fit into, and perhaps enhance, our picture of Brigantian opposition to the Romans and the role of Venutius, former husband of Cartimandua and leader of the anti-Roman forces.[20] It seems generally agreed that the exceptionally large and hurriedly augmented site at Stanwick near Scotch Corner played a part in the attempt to resist Roman campaigning up the Vale of York.[21] It is generally agreed too that Venutius' base lay in the northern half of the loose federation that made up the Brigantes. The North-East on present evidence does not appear to have had a major tribal cult-centre that would have formed a natural focus and power base for opposition to Rome. Stanwick is strategically placed to control the eastern approach to the Stainmore Pass, the natural high corridor to the Eden valley. Moreover, it is along the Stainmore Pass that the typologically early series of marching camps leads away from Stanwick across the summit of the Stainmore Pass and the Rey Cross camp to the Eden valley and towards Carlisle. This is another reason, therefore, for regarding the Carvetii as the centre of Venutius' power base and the prime objective of the governor Cerealis' campaigns in the early seventies.[22]

The boundaries of the canton

What were the boundaries of the Carvetii before, during and
after the Roman occupation? The answers are not necessarily
the same for each period, as we will discover. Nonetheless
some factors are constant, namely the Cumbrian coast to the
west, Alston Edge and the Teesdale moors to the east, and the
Solway Mosses so aptly described by Stukeley as the 'Back
Door to Creation' – to the north.[23] The south-eastern boundary is clear enough in geographic terms with the steep bowl
south of Brough by Stainmore controlling the approach to the
Stainmore Pass discussed above. This may give us an estimate
of the southern boundary too. Shap is relatively close to the
Carvetian heartland and a natural barrier is formed further to
the south by the Tebay Gorge, now followed in spectacular
fashion by the West Coast railwayline and the motorway. Yet
there is one intriguing piece of evidence to suggest that the
canton may have extended further south. A cylindrical milestone from Middleton-in-Lonsdale on the main arterial route
to the South records the distance of fifty-three miles.[24] This
accords closely with the calculable distance to Carlisle along
the road through Tebay to Penrith via Low Borrow Bridge,
Brougham and Old Penrith. If this view is accepted,[25] then it
should imply that the area in question, Upper Lonsdale, also
lay under the administrative control of the Carlisle area at the
time. This probably also means that most of central Lakeland
fell within the same administrative unit. On present evidence
in contrast with the south-eastern uplands around Kirkby
Stephen, it was no more than sparsely populated and therefore appears relatively infrequently in this book. The Barrow
peninsula appears not at all, as it is considered to relate more
to Liverpool Bay and therefore to lie outside the scope of the
present survey. In the north, most commentators suggest that
the extent of the Brigantes, and therefore the Carvetii probably spread beyond the eventual line of Hadrian's Wall.[26] This
is probably correct; the extent of the northern mosses around
the Rivers Esk and Lyne is impressive enough even today after
extensive agricultural reclamation, but further to the north-
west, despite the presence of Lochars Moss, good quality,
well-drained land comes close to the Solway at the southern

end of Annandale. Settlement has now been located in this area on an extensive scale (below p. 74), and it is at least arguable that, with the Solway fordable at certain points as far west as Bowness[27] and beyond, these sites were part of the northern fringe of the Carvetii. If so, their development was cut short by the evolution of the linear barrier on the south side of the Solway in the Hadrianic period. These north Solway sites bear morphological characteristics that at once distinguish them from their far more numerous southern neighbours (below p. 78) and perhaps carry an indication of the late pre-Roman iron age settlement types prior to the Roman occupation.

The people of the Carvetti

While the existence of the *civitas Carvetiorum* is now established, we do not know when it came into formal being as a canton governed by a tribal council, the only known member of which was Flavius Martius from Old Penrith. Unfortunately, his *floruit*, and therefore that of his daughter Martiola, remains in doubt. The cantonal council almost certainly met at Carlisle but it is from other sites, notably Brougham, that persons most likely to have been Carvetian by extraction can be recognised. Annamoris, Vidaris and Ressona are all Celtic names attested at Brougham which give some impression of the indigenous population. To these names we might add Audagus and Baculo from the same place together with Avo from Old Penrith, as well as Tancorix, a lady from Old Carlisle.[28]

The advent of the Romans was naturally a time of considerable mobility. In view of the frequent dedications to Belatucadrus at Brougham, the Lunaris who also appears as a dedicant to Belatucadrus at Carrawburgh may well be identical with the man found commemorating his wife at Brougham. The principal impetus towards social change probably lay in a deliberate policy based on the carrot and the stick that governed the process of Romanisation. We can see it in the social and economic effects of the auxiliary troops perhaps even more than the legionaries attested throughout the region. Auxiliaries from Gaul, Spain, Dalmatia, and the

Low Countries, to mention but a few, exemplified the workings of the Roman system, and the cohort of Baetasians at
Maryport, proudly declaring their acquisition of Roman
citizenship, showed the (potential) advantages that could be
gained. Indeed in a few places we can see the processes at
work on Carvetians. Vidaris, the Carvetian with the Celtic
name from Brougham, set up a memorial to his son Crescenti-
nus, as clear an instance as any of the adoption of latinised
names within the span of a generation. The same process is
probably to be seen in the dedication left at Old Penrith by
Avo for his young son Aurelius. From the same site the
tombstone of M. Cocceius Nonnus, only six years old at the
time of his death, indicates that his father's family had been
granted Roman citizenship by the Emperor Nerva at the very
end of the first century A.D.[29] Such were the mechanics of
Romanisation.

2

History: A.D. 43–367

With the collapse of Cartimandua"'s client kingdom around A.D. 70, the Roman conquest of northern England became a matter of urgency. Cerialis, governor between 71 and 74, campaigned widely in the north, capturing the stronghold at Stanwick. The XXth legion, led by Agricola, must have moved through Carvetian territory at this time, but it was not until Agricola returned as governor in A.D. 78 that permanent forts began to be built here. Cerialis' campaigns are marked largely by marching camps.

Roman marching camps are a direct reflection of the movement of troops on campaign. Particular interest therefore centres on a series of marching camps with the same size or characteristics, such as those of the Agricolan or Severan campaigns in north-eastern Scotland. Another group was long ago noticed as relevant to our area. The marching camps at Rey Cross on the summit of Stainmore, Crackenthorpe near Appleby, and at Plumpton Head, north of Penrith are closely comparable and share the characteristic of having a short, detached rampart and ditch, known as a *tutulus* or *titulum*, blocking the gateways. The evidence is best preserved at Rey Cross, where it is possible to observe the entire layout of the temporary camp and especially its gateways crisply preserved on the moorland, save where limestone quarrying has unfortunately been allowed to destroy the south-western side (Fig. 5). From the stipulations of the Roman military handbook that has come down to us, the size of Rey Cross and its two associated camps is quite sufficient to accommodate a legion. It is probable, as Richmond and McIntyre argued,[1] that the camp is relatively early in type and this increases the prob-

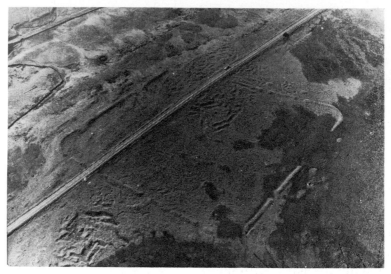

Fig. 5   The early marching camp at Reycross, Stainmore

ability that the legion involved was that engaged in the capture of the Venutian stronghold at Stanwick, a day's march to the east. The two other camps in the series, Crackenthorpe and Plumpton Head, are less well preserved than Rey Cross largely owing to modern agricultural activities but they are separated by a day's march and a further day's progress from Plumpton Head would bring the campaigning army to the Solway crossing at, or near, Carlisle. Whether its ultimate objectives lay beyond Carlisle at this stage is a question that we cannot answer. We do not know whether Venutius was alive or dead by this time or whether he had retreated into the Scottish hills. The Ravenna Cosmography names one place, somewhere between Galloway and Upper Tweedsdale, as *Venutio* but such a name could be coincidence.[2]

The creation of any permanent base at Carlisle was a subject of debate many years ago when the evidence of imported samian pottery was first being applied effectively in establishing a chronology of the northern frontier. The arguments suffered from the absence at that stage of any demonstr-

able early military site at Carlisle. This is no longer the case
and Miss Charlesworth's excavations south of the Castle have
finally identified the defences of a military enclosure that
certainly began life in the seventies, though whether earlier or
later in that decade remains to be seen.[3] For the moment,
however, we are still concerned with temporary, rather than
permanent, installations. The Eden valley is so strategic a
natural corridor that not unnaturally there are several other
marching camps to be found along its length. One of the most
recently discovered lies quite close to Crackenthorpe on the
south side of Kirkby Thore.[4] The camp is interesting for two
reasons; it appears to have been reduced in size, indicating the
dispersal of units on campaign, and its position well away from
the known auxiliary forts and the Roman road suggest that it
belongs early in the sequence of growing control over the Eden
valley. Further north a small temporary camp has been traced
from the air on the north side of the A66 at Brougham (Fig. 8).
Two more examples occur along the arterial road on the shelf
of land north of Old Penrith (Fig. 6), overlooking the east

Fig. 6   A temporary camp near Petteril Green

bank of the River Petteril; several others are known to relate to the construction of Hadrian's Wall and are therefore not discussed here.

The place where one can best appreciate the development of temporary and more permanent arrangements is probably alongside the A66 at Troutbeck at the summit of the pass leading down to Keswick and the heart of northern Lakeland (Fig. 7). Whether a permanent garrison was ever placed in that area remains unlikely on present evidence. On the other hand, the agglomeration of sites at Troutbeck gives us a fascinating glimpse of the way in which considerable bodies of troops came to this natural control point, presumably prior to campaigns into the heart of the massif. The larger of the two marching camps, some thirty nine acres (15.4 ha.) in extent, occupies the highest position of the complex on Lofshaw Hill and was capable, to judge from the size of Rey Cross and other analogous arguments, of holding well over a legion on campaign. The second camp over twelve acres (4.9 ha.) in size lay on the western edge of the crest. The advantages of the position eventually saw the hillcrest crowned by an earth and timber auxiliary fort designed to contol the eastern edge of the northern Lakes. The length of occupation was brief, and the site too exposed to encourage the development of any attached civilian settlement. The role of the short-lived fort, to judge from the likeliest interpretation of the sequence, was taken over by a small fortlet on the northern side of the road that ran past the northern edge of the auxiliary fort.[5]

All these developments probably occurred within the Flavian-Trajanic period during the first or second phases of military occupation and consolidation. As already seen, we now know that during the last two decades of the first century a military site underlay the northern core of Carlisle near the Castle. The principal feature uncovered on the site excavated by Dorothy Charlesworth from 1972–79 is a marvellously preserved timber gateway and timber revetted roadway,[6] comparable in quality to those found at the Valkenberg in Holland (Fig. 27). This military phase is probably to be linked with the presence of a *centurio regionarius* at Carlisle c. A.D. 103, as shown by a writing tablet from Vindolanda.[7] Unfortunate-

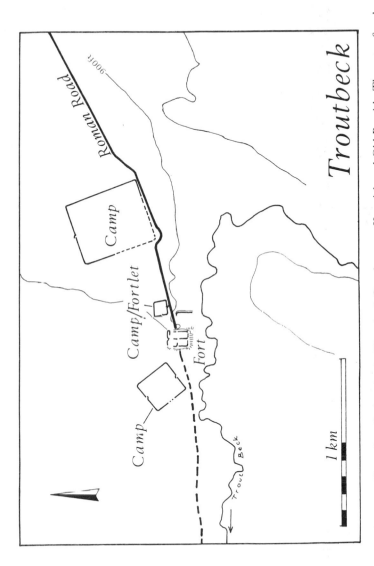

Fig. 7   Roman military installations in the Troutbeck Pass between Keswick and Old Penrith. The rate of replacement underlines the precautions taken during the conquest and garrisoning of the Lake District (after Bellhouse, 1957, and other sources)

ly, Carlisle is one of the few places where anything useful can be said about the early military phase (see further, p. 54). Elsewhere the earliest deposits lie, or are assumed to lie, buried beneath several metres of later deposits on the major fort sites. Old Penrith is the only example to have undergone substantial excavation and there on the south side of the visible remains evidence was found for a defended annexe, or possibly the early fort, dating from some point in the last quarter of the first century. It is presumed that all the Eden valley forts, Brougham, Kirkby Thore and Brough-under-Stainmore go back to a Flavian foundation date, although the presence of Brougham breaks the even spatial distribution of the rest and perhaps, therefore, hints at a rather more complex development sequence. There is sufficient chance evidence from Brough-under-Stainmore to show that the fort controlling the western approaches to the Stainmore Pass was operating in the Flavian period.[8]

On the west the examination of the coin and samian evidence suggests that the forts of the Lake District belong to a later secondary strand of occupation in depth. Most of the scarcely stratified evidence derives from sites to the south such as Watercrook[9] built shortly before A.D. 100, but the presumption is that the brief occupation of the auxiliary fort at Troutbeck discussed above also took place round about the turn of the first century. The later site was clearly related to a road which runs past the fort and can be traced for a short distance further west but its objectives are not clear The little known site at Caermote at the northern end of Bassenthwaite seems designed, like Troutbeck, to control access to the northern Lakes and the lack of a *vicus* suggests, again like Troutbeck, that the length of occupation was limited, with policing reduced to occupation of a fortlet. These two sites are alike in so many ways that they must reflect a co-ordinated response to the problems of policing the Lakes for as long as was thought necessary.

To the south, in the central Lakes, the development of the control road through Ambleside and Hardknott seems linked to the early second century and the development of Ravenglass first as a fortlet, and then as a fort by *c.* A.D. 130 in the late Hadrianic period. Hardknott itself was probably under

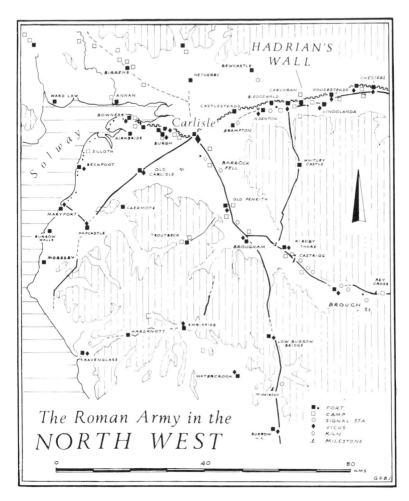

Fig. 8   The Roman military presence in the territory of the Carvetti

construction about the same time to establish an eastward link through Ambleside to Watercrook.[10] To the north of the Lakeland massif, however, the position may have been different owing to the exposed position of the north Cumbrian coast. The strategic defence rested on the Carlisle–Old Car-

lisle–Papcastle road which did not continue to Moresby until
the latter was constructed as part of the additional coastal
defences in A.D. 128–9. The presence of the *ala Augusta* at Old
Carlisle makes it the only attested cavalry unit in this section
of the western command of the Hadrianic defensive system
and stresses the tactical importance of the site's position.
There is as yet, however, no irrefutable evidence for dating the
site prior to the early second century and the same applies to
Papcastle.[11]

This outline survey emphasises the relatively slow build-up
of permanent military dispositions in places other than the
Eden corridor. The lessons of this slow evolution next need to
be applied to understanding the development of the Solway
frontier.

The evolution of the frontier

Hadrian's Wall is probably the most intensively studied
military frontier in the world.[12] In a sense the detailed and
often intensely debated evidence, and the public interest
which it has aroused, have done something of a disservice by
tending to fix the wall in the public imagination as a finite
creation meticulously thought out in detail, and adhering to a
careful strategic plan. Inevitably, therefore, it comes down to
us today as very much a monolithic achievement created at a
moment in time, namely Hadrian's visit to Britain in the
middle of the 120s. In one sense, of course, this is true. On the
other hand comparison with other frontiers in other parts of
the Roman world will show that each frontier in fact evolved
through a number of stages before reaching its final form.
Thus, from analogies elsewhere, we might expect that Hadrian's Wall, particularly in the west with all the problems of
the Solway mosses, underwent several developmental phases.
These have largely evaded our understanding until very
recently, but it is now possible to outline at least some account
of developments in the Trajanic and early Hadrianic period.

In the first place there was a period in the late 70s prior to
any form of integrated frontier that saw the passage of armies
under the leadership of Agricola moving north into lowland
Scotland and beyond. In those years Roman armies fought a

Fig. 9   A temporary camp at Annan

series of campaigns that culminated in A.D. 83 with the climactic victory of *Mons Graupius* and the establishment of Roman military supremacy in north-eastern Scotland. As a prelude to these final campaigns in his fourth season Agricola campaigned in the area facing Ireland, and indeed entered into political negotiations with an exiled Irish chieftain. A cryptic passage in Tacitus *Agricola* 24 referring to this event is nowadays more often than not taken to refer to campaigning beyond the Forth of Clyde. The older interpretation, however, implied that the campaign in question ranged across Galloway and the Stewartry towards Stranraer and the Ayrshire coast. Indeed there is still much to be said for this approach, particularly since the recent discovery of a Roman marching camp at Girvan on the west coast.

In this context the Roman occupation of Carlisle clearly seems to lie within a few years of A.D. 80, but in assessing the early northward campaigns along the west coast route we should remember the tactical disadvantage of Carlisle's position at the southern end of an extremely large area of moss stretching towards Gretna Green. Seaborne landing of men on the south Dumfriesshire coast had the advantage of offering rapid communication, either up the valley of the Annan or the valley of the Nith. Two auxiliary forts lie at the bottom of each valley, at Annan Foot (Fig. 9) and Ward Law (Fig. 10) respectively, but auxiliary forts are not marching camps

Fig. 10   The hillfort and Roman fort at Ward Law

which directly relate to the movement of men on campaign. In 1977, however, the first of such a series of camps was discovered at Annan Foot, where a nine-acre marching camp was located at the tidal limit of the Annan.[13] It lies within a larger defensive ditch related to the riverbank, perhaps indicating the presence of a trans-shipment bridgehead. Clearly it played a role in the movement of troops forward either into Annandale or along the easy hillslopes by Ruthwell towards Dumfries and the valley of the Nith. By *c.* A.D. 112 Annandale's population appears to have undergone a census implying incorporation within the Roman system whether as an outlying independent tribe, or not.[14]

At the moment therefore this is all that can be said about the earliest phase of military history amongst the Carvetii. Most of the auxiliary forts are assumed to have Flavian origins but this has been proved in very few places. At Carlisle a military base of unproven size is known to lie at the south side of the castle following excavations first by Charlesworth and then by the Carlisle Archaeological Unit. The remarkably preserved timber structure of the south gate along with its associated rampart and roadway have been uncovered in recent years. The site continued in apparently military occupation into the late second century, but from the earlier period tile stamps belonging to the second, ninth and twentieth legions have been recovered and set an intriguing question as to the nature of the garrison in the late Flavian/Trajanic period.

A tantalising passage in the Vindolanda tablets attests the presence of a *centurio regionarius* at Carlisle in A.D. 103.[15] This should mean that the body of troops stationed at Carlisle formed part of what has been called the Stanegate Frontier, a term first proposed some forty years ago to describe the frontier arrangements prior to the creation of Hadrian's Wall. The Stanegate proper is the medieval name for the Roman arterial road which ran behind Hadrian's Wall along its central sector and was known to have a sequence of military posts along it. They included such sites as Old Church (Brampton), Nether Denton, Throp and *Vindolanda*. On this basis some scholars have suggested that the Stanegate represented an open frontier articulated along an arterial road with alternating large and small forts. The problem, as others have subsequently pointed out, was that this sytem, if it existed at all (and the evidence often rests on relatively outdated excavations such as those on the fortlet at Haltwhistle Common), lacked any substance either to the east or west of the central section. In recent years, however, the fort discovered from the air at Washing Well, on Gateshead Common, is generally agreed to form some part of an east-west extension involving Corbridge and a road alignment along the south side of the Tyne.[16] To the east, however, the presence of urban Tyneside is a major impediment to increasing our knowledge. It always appeared likely that, if this system was to be shown to exist under Trajan or the early years of Hadrian's reign, then the evidence would come from the west.

This indeed it began to do in 1977, when a kilometre or so behind Hadrian's Wall, and on top of a commanding hill behind Burgh village, traces of a fort (Fig. 11) appeared that proved to belong to the Trajanic and early Hadrianic phase.[17]

Fig. 11   The Stanegate fort at Burgh-by-Sands

It could therefore be assumed to be the first stage of a westward system from Carlisle to the Solway mosses. The presence of a pre-Hadrianic fort at Burgh-by-Sands, helped accommodate the isolated evidence already available from study of the auxiliary fort at Kirkbride on the edge of the tidal limit of the River Wampool. Pottery of the period around A.D. 100–115 consistently appeared in an area which is now known to form a four-and-a-half to five-acre auxiliary fort. Aerial photography over the last few years has shown that a road alignment ran due east from Kirkbride towards Burgh-by-Sands and this, it can be argued, forms the western extension of the Stanegate system. But the story does not stop there. The presence of these forts implied staging points some six miles apart, and in 1979, along the line of the road, further evidence appeared with a series of discoveries near Finglandrigg, west of Kirkbampton.[18] The sites relate to a whalebacked ridge commanding very extensive views, far greater than those from Drumburgh, located on a small drumlin one and a half miles to the north.

With these newly-discovered sites, other features also appeared. Returning to Burgh-by-Sands, amongst the aerial photographic evidence for the fort, there also occurred the telltale circular cropmark of what on excavation appeared to be a watch-tower or guard-post some 19 metres across, containing a timber tower forming part of the gate. This in turn was associated with a palisade and ditch which could be seen running across the ridge, to the south of the village of Burgh-by-Sands and the ford of the Sandwath at Sandsfield further to the north. It was there, in 1307, that Edward I died leading the English army against Robert the Bruce. This historical event highlights the topographical importance of the route again emphasised by the large size of the garrison attested at the later fort of Burgh-by-Sands in the Roman period. The presence of the palisaded ditch and watch-tower, both preceding the auxiliary fort, again belonging to the period round about A.D. 100, shows the development of defences on the *clausura* pattern familiar in other parts of the Roman empire. The running ditch forming the next section to the west was located and excavated in 1982 along the crest of Far Hill, overlooking the great embayment of Burgh Marsh; which was far more extensive till drained in the last century.

Already in 1979 excavation on one of a series of related analagous features had begun at Easton on the opposite, western side of the marsh, halfway between Burgh and Kirkbridge (see above). This indeed showed further elements of a similar system. A small circular site 19 m. across, again proved to be not a minute native farm but a circular watch-tower containing a tower built into the enclosing rampart

(Fig. 12). From it thére ran, in the second period of the
structure's existence, a palisaded ditch that ascended the
ridge towards another site at Fingland Rigg some ¾ kilometres
away. On the ridge it is possible to trace both the Stanegate
and the probable continuation of the palisaded ditch in front
of it for some considerable distance. There is no space to
describe the details here but we may conclude that the
palisade and ditch system was not a special development
specifically related to the approaches to the Sandwath and

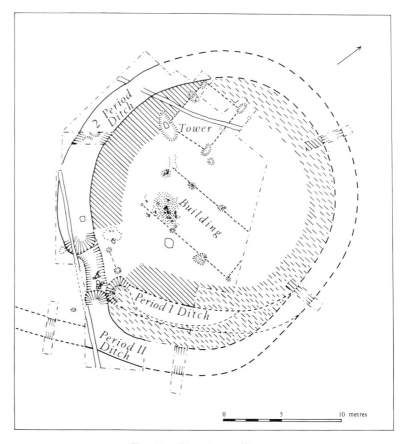

Fig. 12   The site at Easton

Burgh-by-Sands but more probably a linking feature of the
proto-frontier arrangements, where mossland did not inter-
vene. The work of checking air photographic evidence continues, and further lengths of the palisade and ditch will
emerge in this way. Meanwhile, although this fresh evidence
deriving from aerial photography has yet to be exhausted, it
does give us, when carefully checked on the ground through
excavation, a thoroughly new view of the way in which a
coastal defence was developing in the years preceding the
actual construction of Hadrian's Wall. In this Stanegate
period advantage was taken of the mosses to run an intermit-
tent defence closely related to watch-towers and forts some-
way back from the actual line of the coast. In this way
Burgh-by-Sands I preceded Burgh-by-Sands II, and Kirkbride preceded Bowness (Fig. 13). While still further forts
may emerge to the west, the importance of Kirkbride must
be recognised as the probable terminal of the main system and
an important port.[19]

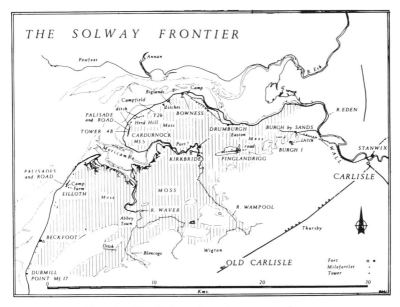

Fig. 13   The Solway Frontier : general map.

Hadrianic Coastal Defences

Although the precise date when Hadrian's Wall was established in the coastal zone remains in doubt, one may like to see this development as representing occupation of the actual coastal line in depth. The familiar turf wall and vallum system was run through as far as Bowness-on-Solway. The original turf wall was succeeded by a stone-built version at a date that is a matter of debate depending on the interpretation of the pottery from the Solway House (Milecastle 79) excavations.[20] Beyond Bowness, and across Moricambe, for the best part of a century elements of an associated defence system have been found along the Cumbrian coast. In the 1870s the antiquarian Ferguson recorded the presence of stone towers and a certain number of milefortlets, as they were termed, but it was not until 1928 that Collingwood published his realisation that the disjointed remains in fact formed part of an alternating system of milefortlets and towers imitating the spacing of milecastles and turrets on Hadrian's Wall proper. With this basis it was possible for Bellhouse to carry out important work in infilling our knowledge of the towers and milefortlets, notably in the Silloth and Cardurnock areas.[21] Yet there still remained room for further advances in our knowledge. The exceedingly sharp early drought in 1975 in this area showed that two parallel ditches running on to the rear and front defences of Milefortlet 1 (Biglands) created a double-ditch cordon in which the isolated coastal towers actually sat. This was, of course, a much more logical system, rendering the isolated towers not simply hostages to fortune, but part of an integrated linear defence along the foreshore. Severn Valley ware found in the rearward ditch at Milefortlet 1 (Biglands) shows that the defence probably only operated for a relatively short period in the early years of the full Hadrian's Wall system.[22]

Yet again, comparison with other frontiers, particularly in Germany raised the question of whether the stone towers were in fact the first to exist at the relevant points. Elsewhere timber towers often preceded their stone equivalents; on the Taunus frontier in Germany, for instance, they are often still partly visible alongside their stone successors. The question was settled at Tower 4B behind Cardurnock village where area excavation on the measured position of the tower produced the evidence not of the stone structure (which was eventually found some 11 metres to the north) but of a timber-built tower or platform associated with a frontal palisade (Fig. 14). A clay and cobble platform measuring some 4.45 m. × 3.45 m. had been laid on the natural sand.

Fig. 14   Cardurnock Tower 4B under excavation

Around its periphery ran a construction trench which was joined at the front by slots running in from either side to form a continuous trench. Examination of this showed that it had been cut by gang work and that it contained the sumps of a wooden palisade that had run flush up with the front of the tower or guard platform implied by the presence of the clay and cobble base. The tower was soon replaced. A second palisade ran through the dismantled platform and this showed that in a second stage more emphasis was placed on manpower in the milefortlets. The third structural phase involved an isolated stone tower, long paralleled elsewhere, actually built over the forward ditch of the earlier defences. While the relative sequence of structures is clear, the absolute dating is not (below, p. 38).

At Cardurnock, the estuary of Moricambe, the joint channels of the Waver and the Wampool create a major break in the shore line before Grune Point and towards Silloth. It was on the north side of Silloth that a series of excavations produced further corroborative evidence to show the presence of a coastal palisade (Fig. 15). Like the excavations at Cardurnock the work showed that the palisade, which because of the extremely sandy soil lacked any form of associated

Fig. 15   The coastal defences at Silloth – the base of a palisade

ditch, had gone through two distinct phases, one palisade being replaced by another. Structurally, it was of exceptional interest because the original bedding trench had been cut into the sand and then rammed full of redband clay, probably transported from Dubmill Point, some six miles to the south. In this way it proved possible to bed the palisading in a firmer manner than would normally have been possible in the extremely sandy subsoil. The patrol road running to the rear of this defensive system bends inwards to touch on a small temporary camp. The camp itself was overlaid by the remains of a field system belonging to a small farm that grew up presumably to supply the mile fortlet in this area, now lost beneath the modern town of Silloth.[23]

We therefore have a substantially more logical view of the Solway coastal defences as an integrated linear barrier in the early stages of its evolution (Fig. 16). The system still rested

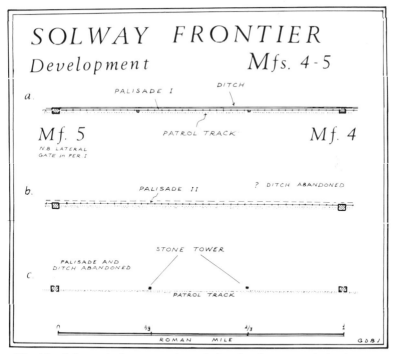

Fig. 16   Schematic interpretation of the development of the Solway defences

Fig. 17   The Roman fort at Maryport

on the major forts of Beckfoot, which appears in many years as
a magnificent cropmark site on the coastal dunes, and of
Maryport, the site of which goes on into at least the fourth
century, and may well have been the command base for
whatever fleet unit was operating in this section of the Solway
Firth. Maryport itself is known from excavation to be a
Hadrianic foundation and the life of the fort extends through
into the second half of the fourth century (Fig. 17). Further
south, the existence of forts is known at Burrow Walls,
Workington and again, on a hill overlooking the sea at
Moresby. Neither site has been extensively excavated and it
would be premature to say anything of their detailed history.
Nothing is known of coastal milefortlets south of Maryport
and the question of a southward extension of such a system
remains a highly debated issue. The latest air photographic
evidence suggests the presence of a milefortlet south of the
Workington conurbation and, if this is confirmed by excavation, then a series of milefortlets probably extended at least as
far south as St. Bees Head.

The frontier in the mid second century and after

The details of Hadrian's Wall (Fig. 18) have been intensively studied and several up-to-date accounts render a detailed description of the remains unnecessary in this context where space is at a premium.[24] Instead it is more relevant here to examine the problems that remain. The line of the Wall ran off the Whin Sill at the crossing of the River Irthing, east of Birdoswald, and dropped down towards Castlesteads over Pike and Hare Hills. It then continued across the marshy northern side of the Eden Plain north of Carlisle Airport and High Crosby to the largest fort on the Wall at Stanwix, the northern suburb of Carlisle. West of the Irthing crossing, the original plan of the Wall saw its construction in turf, later to be replaced with the familiar stone curtain built to an intermediate guage. In places where it has been examined the stone curtain was found to be laid directly on its turf predecessor. The great exception to this occurs immediately west of the Irthing, in the Birdoswald sector between Harrow Scar (Milecastle 49) and Milecastle 51 (near Appletrees). Over this section the two Walls take a different course, as they do again very marginally five kilometres further west at Garthside. Much interest therefore focussed on the date of the Turf Wall milecastle (M/C 50 TW) and its stone-built successor slightly to the north. Both produced building inscriptions of the emperor Hadrian, the Turf Wall milecastle appropriately yielding a remarkable fragment of an inscription cut in timber with its letters inlaid in red paint.[25] The Birdoswald sector, therefore, showed that there at any rate the replacement of the turf wall by its stone successor had occurred prior to A.D. 138 and on general probability earlier rather than later in Hadrian's reign.

How far this picture can be applied to the remaining western sector of the Wall remains in doubt. At present we are dependent on the interpretation of the pottery evidence from Milecastle 79, superimposed turf and stone structures one Roman mile short of Bowness. In their report the excavators thought there was a significant difference between the pottery recovered from the early period at Milecastle 79 and the previous work at Milecastle 50 (Turf Wall), the only other

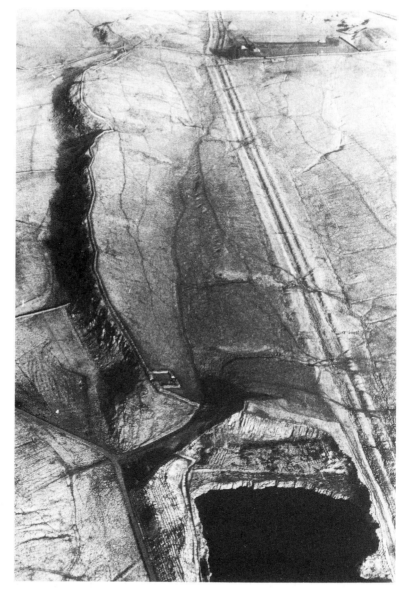

Fig. 18 Hadrian's Wall and the Vallum at Cawfields

milecastle to be examined in the western sector. Because the volume of pottery recovered from the Solway site was approximately double that recovered from Milecastle 50, they argued for a more extended occupation. This was further supported by a general absence of typologically early pottery on the Solway site with the creation of the Antonine Wall in A.D. 142 offering a *terminus ante quem*. This suggests that the stone reconstruction of the Solway sector lagged behind replacement of the earth and timber structures in the west central sector. Indeed it was suggested that one sherd of samian pottery stratigraphically placed in an intermediate position between the superimposed turf and stone milecastles should be dated to the A.D. 160s. This might mean that the stone replacement did not occur until as late as the partial refurbishing of the Wall defences under, or shortly after, the governor Calpurnius Agricola.[26]

Until there is considerably more evidence from the western sector, it would be dangerous to base such an argument on a single sherd. When set beside some of the new evidence that is emerging the broad historical point does, however, seem to be established for a drawn-out transitional phase. It is often forgotten that the strategically placed fort of Carvoran was being rebuilt in stone as late as A.D. 136–7. Either the site had been abandoned and was being resuscitated very late in the Hadrianic period or, more likely, the presumed Stanegate fort on the site was very slow to be refurbished in stone. An analogous situation may perhaps also be inferred (allowing for physical transition of sites) at Burgh-by-Sands I and II. The pottery from the former contains types that may protract the date of transition well into the Hadrianic period. The problem of transition from earth and timber to stone-built forts is complicated in this area, where no good building stone is readily available, and it should be remembered that the Hadrianic fort at Bowness on Solway, the terminal fort of the stone curtain and the second largest site on the whole Wall, was timber-built in its initial phase. More surprisingly, the same seems to be true of the outpost fort of Bewcastle.[27]

We may now turn to the Solway coastal sector. The continuing pattern of milefortlets and towers has already been discussed (p. 30), and the overall date of the layout, whether earlier or later in the Hadrianic sequence, is not in question; the chronology and other aspects are. The body of material on which one can attempt to generalise is not great. There is evidence from excavation at nine milefortlets and nine stone-built, as opposed to timber, towers. In most cases the excavations were primarily locational or salvage operations[28] and at only two sites, Biglands and Cardurnock (Milefortlets 1 and 5 respectively), were large areas investigated.[29] It is clear from the evidence available that there is considerable variation in size, and indeed between sizes at different periods, as shown at the two above mentioned sites where substantial excavation took place. Cardurnock (Fig. 19) appears to be paralleled by a similarly large site on the south side of the Moricambe estuary at Skinburness and such a sensitive strategic position was always likely to be well protected at times when the frontier was actively held. Antonine re-occupation is attested at Cardurnock, Milefortlets 9, 16 and 22 and Towers 12A, 12B, 15A and 16B where ceramic evidence or indications of rebuilding have been forthcoming.[30]

Fig. 19   The milefortlet at Cardurnock

The evidence at Biglands suggests that the re-occupation occurred twice after the two abandonments of the Antonine Wall and therefore that the main periods of occupation effectively span the second century. This can be brought into accord with the structural evidence from the linear defence which also indicates a three period sequence. During this sequence, as we have seen (p. 31), manning of the timber towers with the running palisade and ditch saw the abandonment first of the former then the latter and their third-phase replacement by milefortlets and isolated stone-built towers. The evidence from both milefortlets and linear defences in at least the Bowness–Cardurnock sector is mutually confirmative.

While there is now a growing body of information available from the coastal sites, the same cannot be said of the sites in the hinterland. There has been no excavation within the forts at Old Carlisle (Fig. 29), Old Penrith, and Brougham, arguably three of the most important sites in the area, and relatively small investigations at Papcastle, Kirkby Thore and Brough-under-Stainmore.[31] The sample of evidence is far too small on which to base generalisation; indeed, even if extensive modern excavation were to take place on one of the sites of the interior, the lessons of fifty years work on the sites of Roman Wales has shown the dangers inherent in attempting historical generalisations from one or two forts. This is particularly true of the Eden valley, where forts were always likely, both before and after Hadrian, to serve as bases for a strategic reserve on the northern frontier. As the evidence currently stands we have to place the emphasis of historical interpretation not on excavation but on numismatic or epigraphic evidence, where available.

It is, for example, difficult to judge the effect of the probable evacuation of troops attendant upon the abandonment of the Hadrianic barrier and the construction of the Antonine Wall in A.D. 142. Reduction of a fort to care-and-maintenance is not susceptible to easy archaeological detection and many of the sites along the Eden corridor must have been retained under some form of military control, even if only as oversize posting stations along the arterial road to the south. After the final abandonment of the Antonine Wall there is some evidence for the refurbishing that one might expect, certainly at Watercrook and Ribchester far to the south, and less definitely at Hardknott in the Lakeland massif. The confused period of attack and counter-attack across the northern frontier that saw the intervention of Ulpius Marcellus in the A.D. 180s must have affected the north-western frontier area considerably but in ways about which we can currently only speculate (Fig. 20). The clearest evidence available at the

Fig. 20   Two superimposed temporary camps at Brackenrigg which probably formed the construction centre for the western end of the wall system behind Bowness

moment comes from the coastal sites, where as already described, the re-occupation of the milefortlets, notably Biglands and Cardurnock, appears to relate to successive abandonments of the Antonine Wall and therefore lie within the second century. Abandonment followed apparently but at one coastal fort well to the south at Ravenglass destruction by enemy action occurred sometime around the Severan period.[32]

The coastal sites were, of course, vulnerable to localised sea raiding and the emphasis of defensive methods was changing, as the nature of frontier defence was itself changing, away from intensive occupation by large but dispersed manpower towards the greater use of troops deployed from a limited number of strongpoints. Such a picture does not emerge along the Cumbrian coast till late in the fourth century. The forts of Beckfoot, Burrow Walls and Moresby have yielded sufficient evidence to make this point. The excavations at Maryport and Ravenglass where substantial areas of the interior were investigated prove it beyond doubt.[33] At both sites there is plentiful evidence for late fourth century occupation and this may also imply a limited re-activation of the more strategically placed milefortlets such as Cardurnock (Milefortlet 5) where, like Milefortlets 12 and 20, some fourth century material has been recovered. The overall setting of these developments is more fully discussed in the final chapter of this book.

3

Communications and Urban Settlement

The backbone of communication within the tribal area was formed by the arterial road now roughly followed by the line of the A6, along the valley of the Petteril between Carlisle and Penrith.[1] At Penrith the road divided into two further strategic lines. The more famous is that which runs from Scotch Corner near Catterick, across the Stainmore Pass, and down into the upper Eden Valley to Brough-under-Stainmore, and thence along the north side of the valley through Kirkby Thore to the junction of the two road systems at Brougham outside Penrith. The southerly route out of the tribal area is roughly marked by the present line of the M6 through the Lune Gap at Tebay, a line abandoned in the medieval period because of the importance of Kendal, but followed by the west coast rail route in the last century. The northern tip of this road is only sketchily known north of the important farm sites in Crosby Ravensworth, and there is a possibility that the road forked to join the Maiden Way at Kirkby Thore.[2] The latter was a well engineered, strategic route followed by no modern communications but which in the Roman period served to link the Eden Valley across the mountainous terrain of Alston Ridge to the central section of Hadrian's Wall at Carvoran. The information available about the only known intermediate fort at Whitley Castle suggests that lead extraction may be another reason for the road's existence (p. 119).

The multiplicity of military sites along the Stainmore/Eden Valley suggests that we have a great deal to learn about the military history involved. Certainly it is unlikely that all the fort sites can have been occupied simultaneously. This may explain why the two known roads leaving the central Lake District derive from separate forts at Old Penrith and

Brougham. From the latter ran the route known as High Street which developed along the line of the ridges to the east of Ullswater and descended to the fort at Ambleside on Lake Windermere. From there the route continued through the Wrynose and Hardknott Passes to the well-known fort at Hardknott, connecting the route down Eskdale to the fort at Ravenglass. The second westerly route was long known in essentials to antiquarians but has only recently been re-surveyed.[3] It ran across broken country south-west from Old Penrith to the crest of the pass at Troutbeck where the previously known marching camps have recently been found to surround an auxiliary fort (p. 18). From the top of the pass the line dropped down in the direction of Keswick, but the details of its course remain uncertain after the first kilometre or so. This is unfortunate because there is the possibility, rather than the probability, of an auxiliary fort lying in the heart of the Lake District near Derwentwater. Whatever the case may be, the line is assumed to have run on to the important comunications point at Papcastle near Whitehaven where an auxiliary fort guarded the western approaches to the central Lake District in much the same way that Troutbeck did to the east.

The easiest approach to Papcastle, however, lay along the Solway Plain where a major road, now largely followed by the A595, ran south-east through Old Carlisle, past Papcastle and on to the southern side of the Cumbrian coast defences at Moresby, south of Workington. The other approach to this site lay along the little-known road that linked the Cumbrian coastal defensive system. This road ran north through Burrow Walls, Maryport (which was linked to Papcastle by a short connecting road) and Beckfoot, though little of its visible remains has ever been recovered. North of Beckfoot, recent work on the Solway coastal defences has identified part of the lateral communication road behind the defensive palisade now known at Silloth. The patrol road presumably ran out to the tip of Skinburness where the estuary of Moricambe can still be forded at low tide. Between Milefortlet 5 and Bowness the coastal road, as identified in the last century, has again been observed recently behind the frontal ditch system now known to link the milefortlets (p. 30). East of Bowness little is known of the road that must have run to the rear of Hadrian's Wall.

In this context the position of the Roman fort at Kirkbride appears anomalous. It controlled the crossing of the River Wampool and was connected by two short link roads across the moss to both Bowness and Drumburgh. The date of the site, however, is known to lie principally within the Trajanic period, thus raising the question of its relationship to the Stanegate phase in the build-up to Hadrian's Wall. In fact, recent air photographic work has discovered clear evidence of a road running eastwards from the site for several kilometres to the newly discovered fort at Fingland Rigg (above, p. 28) and flanked by numerous small farming settlements. Its destination can only have been Carlisle and this route represents the western extension of the Stanegate in the early years of the second century A.D.

While Carlisle remained a port, albeit difficult of access, into the nineteenth century, the importance of Bowness as the terminal of the mural barrier of Hadrian's Wall is easily explained in relation to the Solway. There are currently three points at which the estuary can be forded in the Bowness/Port Carlisle area. Conventional communication with the Dumfries area in the Roman period lay, however, via the line of the arterial road running due north from Carlisle and crossing the Esk at Netherby. There, close to the area of the Debatable Lands, the road must have turned due west to a well-defined route through Birrens, past Burnswark, and so to Annandale and Nithsdale. The route was a difficult one on the mosses north of Carlisle and represents a substantial deviation east of the modern road and railway line through Gretna Green. This may mean that sea crossings were more important than we now realise. The Roman fort at Ward Law must have controlled a harbour at the mouth of the Nith estuary, and air photography has recently established a substantial number of native sites accompanying the known military fort and fortlets up the valley (p. 74).

The signal stations

As befits a frontier zone, however, roads were not the only means of communication, particularly on the west central sector of the Wall and on the Stainmore Pass and its approaches. The existence of a Roman arterial signalling system in the Upper Eden Valley was first noted by Richmond[4] who analysed the probable interrelationship of several of its components, particularly Maiden Castle and Roper Castle, in the central section of the Stainmore Pass. At the time, his article was probably intended as a preliminary statement because Richmond was aware of another signal station near Appleby (below, p. 49) and of the large gaps separating several known sites, in particular the fort at Brough-under-Stainmore and Maiden Castle. Recent aerial survey and fieldwork has enabled us to increase the number of known sites and offer a more complete corpus of evidence for the signalling system, notably on the western ascent to Stainmore (fig. 21).

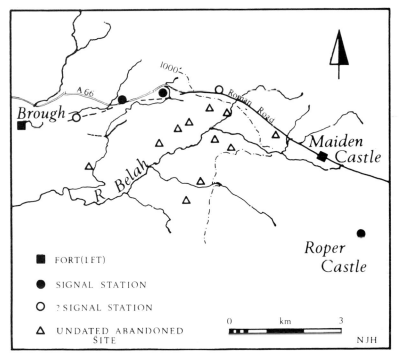

Fig. 21   The signalling system in the Western Approach to the Stainmore Pass

The Eden Valley can be divided into a number of separate environmental blocks, distinguished by the relative availability of arable land. Between Carlisle and Penrith, the Roman road passes close to several unploughed fells that have preserved known signal stations at Barrock Side and Barrock Fell.[5] These, it should be said, do not share the same form as those on the Stainmore and their contemporaneity remains in doubt. The Penrith area, on the other hand, has been subject to heavy agricultural activity in the post-Roman period, and no signal station sites were known until aerial survey in 1976. South of Kirkby Thore, agricultural land gradually gives way to pasture, until, on Stainmore, little or no arable exists. It is this area that lends itself best to fieldwork.

As Richmond recognised, Roper Castle represents the top of the Stainmore Pass signalling system, although arguments about its precise plan, whether square with rounded corners or simply round, remain subjective. It is closely comparable in shape and size to the other examples now known, roughly 30 m. in total diameter, with a circular central mound surrounded by two ditches. From the signal tower at Roper Castle the fortlet at Maiden Castle is intervisible and Richmond suggested that the latter site should be seen as integral to the signalling system. No alternative site for a signalling station has been found after intensive survey in the immediate vicinity and there seems no alternative but to treat Maiden Castle as fulfilling in part such a function. There is a difficulty in that only third or fourth century finds have been made on the site, whereas the signalling system must in origin at any rate be far earlier. In any case, the site is rarely intervisible with Brough fort, some 8 km. to the west, due to poor local visibility and low cloud, and intervening signalling positions are obviously still to seek.

On Slapestone, near Palliard Bridge, 1½ km. west of Maiden Castle, are the remains of a settlement of Romano-British type, occupying a wind hollow close to 1240 ft. above O.D.; but no remains of a signal station are visible. The nearest example discovered lies on Johnson's Plain, 3½ km. north-west of Maiden Castle, strategically placed above the point where the road (following the probable line of the Roman road) turns westward, and it is intervisible with Maiden Castle. The site is less well preserved than several of the others, and the central mound and encircling ditches broken by an entrance to the south are best seen from the air.

Only 1½ km. west lies one of the best preserved of the signal stations, at the Punchbowl Inn, occupying the summit of a natural hill (Fig. 22). This site is clearly intervisible with the Johnson's Plain example, but not with Maiden Castle. It was surveyed on the ground in 1975. The south facing entrance suggests the Roman road ran along the valley of the Powbrand Syke, 300 m. south of the modern line.

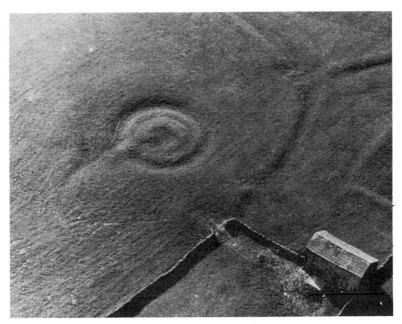

Fig. 22   Signal station at the Punchbowl Inn, Stainmore

A little over one kilometre to the west lies the next example, on the steep hill above Augill Bridge and clearly visible from the previous site (Fig. 23). The station is again well preserved as an earthwork, although it has been cut by a ditch associated with post-medieval enclosures. This site was chosen for a test excavation in 1975, when a quadrant was cut in the

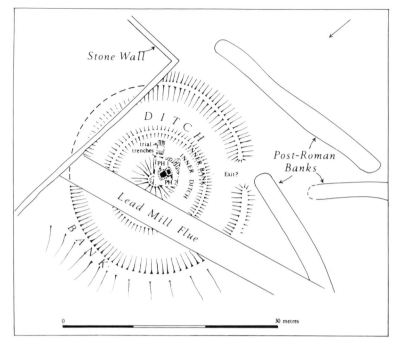

Fig. 23   The signal station at Augill Bridge, Stainmore

central mound which was composed of reddish clay not natural to the site. One of the four post holes of the tower supports was located and was found to be square. The post hole had been re-cut for a second phase when a circular, slighter post was used. The approach ramp was uncovered towards the south-west, revetted by stones. A section was dug across the inner ditch in waterlogged conditions and a number of burnt food bones extracted, all from cattle.[6] This excavation proved the function of the earthwork beyond reasonable doubt, and provided a starting point for the eventual total excavation of a signal station.

West of Augill Bridge, the Upper Eden Valley is dominated by a boulder clay terrain which has been subjected to successive ploughing in the post-Roman period, to such an extent that the course of the Roman road is still a matter for conjecture in the vicinity of Brough fort. Given that it passed south of the Punchbowl Inn site and of the Augill Bridge station, the most sensible course would seem to be via the south bank of the Augill Beck via Battle Hill to Church Brough. Recent fieldwork has identified a road following this course and has also located the probable site of the last signal station between Augill Bridge and Brough fort, 400 m. north of Augill Castle on Battle Hill. This site is only visible in the winter as a shallow saucer in pasture, about 30 m. in diameter, but summer weed growth picks out the ditches, and an unusually vigorous nettle patch occupies the supposed central mound. There is clear visibility between this and the Augill Beck signal station 1½ km. away, and between it and Brough fort, 1½ km. away and 50 m. lower. A deep cut in Battle Hill immediately south of the probable signal station perhaps marks the line of the Roman road, but alternative routes have been suggested, such as the line of the Maiden Way still visible north of Villa Park for 600 m., and perhaps running west to Brough Castle via Augill Castle.[7]

West of Brough, modern ploughing has totally destroyed the system, which probably followed the road and is now lost in the military installations of the Warcop Firing Range north of the A66. In any case no new examples have been located between Brough and Brackenber, on Appleby Golf Course. There, a probable site was mentioned by Richmond[8] but never published by its discoverer, the late James McIntyre. The Brackenber site is relatively low-lying but exploits the comparatively good visibility of the dry valley looking north-west towards Brampton, and eastwards to Gateshede, whence Vicarage Bank, Warcop, or one of the other hills in that vicinity is visible. The site is well preserved, presumably because of the low fertility of the sandy soil which has never been ploughed. It is round, with an entrance towards the east, and two ditches and counterscarp banks, of which the outer has been levelled (Fig. 24).

To the north-west the next probable area for a signal station lies on the ridge close to Gale House north-east of Appleby Extensive medieval strip cultivation at this point has probably removed all surface trace of the expected feature. Another station may have occurred at another high point near Hang-

Fig. 24   The signal station at Brackenber Moor

ingshaw further along the ridge before more definite evidence
recurs at Castrigg. There a small fortlet has long been known
and aerial survey[9] additionally revealed a circular ditched site
similar to the examples from Stainmore. The presence of the
fortlet and signal station alongside one another points to their
non-contemporaneity and emphasises the long historical
sequence involved in the build-up of installations along the
Eden Valley. The presence of fortlets like Castrigg and
Maiden Castle may eventually be explained by hiatus in the
occupation of the main auxiliary forts. North of Brougham
there is again crop mark evidence to suggest the presence of a
signalling station alongside the Roman road on the high
ground at Bleak House north of Penrith. The site was very
skilfully chosen to enable a tower to command a view both
down to Brougham on the River Eamont and up the line of the
road to Carlisle now effectively followed by the A6. The
northward links in the system may eventually emerge from
further fieldwork.

One further site needs to be discussed here. The existence of the signalling system along the Eden corridor had long been implied, if not fully understood. Yet the Eden valley route is not the only strategic communication corridor in the area. The west coast route running up Lonsdale through the Tebay gap was also of considerable importance. At the head of Lonsdale near Sedbergh a projecting spur beside the Roman road near Middleton Hall bears indication of the former presence of a sub-rectangular native farm. To one side stands a small circular feature with a single ditch and counterscarp very similar to the Stainmore signal stations (Fig. 25). Previously it has been interpreted as a barrow but a break in the ditch circuit makes this unlikely and, taking its superb

Fig. 25   Possible signal station at Middleton Hall apparently associated
with a 'native' settlement site

position into account, it is far likelier to represent another signal station on the Stainmore model. Although standing in isolation for the moment, this example suggests the existence of a second arterial signalling system along the west coast passing information to and from Lancaster and the south.

The civitas capital

During recent years archaeologists have come to realise that
many of the answers to the history of the northern frontier can
only derive from excavation at Carlisle. The presence of the
major Roman fort of Stanwix on the northern side of the river
has, of course, long been known. Although the site lies buried
beneath the modern road, the church and a recreational area,
some of its plan has been established in outline from limited
excavation. Documentary sources indicate that the garrison
concerned was of milliary size (just short of a thousand men),
an exceptional number that suggests that is was the location of
the command centre of at least the west-central and western
side of the Wall. The site is known to have housed the *ala
Petriana*, the cavalry unit nearly a thousand strong whose
presence strengthens the argument for regarding Carlisle as a
command centre.

Yet the presence of a large fort at Stanwix is only one facet
of the archaeology of the city. Prior to the construction of the
Wall, the military base controlling the river crossing would
more logically have lain to the south under the present city.
The general interpretation, according to St. Cuthbert writing
in A.D. 685, is that the core of the present city (Fig. 26)
marked the site of a Roman town of some seventy acres. The
saint also recorded the survival of the fountain in working
order which presumably implies that the water supply system
established in the Roman period was still functioning. More
intriguingly still, he conducted his business with a *praepositus*,
possibly an official holding a post that had survived from the
Roman period.

This evidence points to the existence of a major settlement
on the south bank of the river in the Roman period. The
position of Carlisle as a border city has meant that the
settlement has enjoyed almost continuous occupation ever
since and the quantity and quality of its medieval town plans
make the city a uniquely well-documented site. The area of
the Lanes along Scotch Street preserves elements of many
medieval property divisions to this day, but far less can be
elucidated of the Roman period. Unfortunately archaeological
work is still at the stage where, although progressing, it cannot

Fig. 26 Aerial view of Carlisle from the north

offer any definitive analysis of the development of the area
south of the river. It seems logical that the large civilian
walled town seen by Saint Cuthbert took advantage of the
natural bank now sealed beneath the West walls, north of the
railway station. Logically too, it was preceded by a military
establishment in the years prior to the construction of Hadrian's Wall. Indeed the discovery of tiles bearing the stamp of
the Ninth Legion from Scalesceugh a few kilometres south of
Carlisle makes it very likely that the legion or, more probably,
a vexillation of it was involved at Carlisle. The discovery of a
wooden writing tablet relating to the year AD. 103 at *Vindolanda* has also helped. It attests the presence of a *centurio
regionarius* at *Luguvalium*, the place name being readily de-
cipherable and referring not to Stanwix on the north side of
the river but to the establishment on the south. What form
this took is the principal problem that the archaeologist faces
today.[10]

   In 1892 excavation in the grounds of Tullie House Museum
produced the remains of a timber-built structure measuring
67 m. × 12 m. in a remarkable state of preservation. It ran
along an approximately north-east,, south-west alignment
under the southern edge of Tullie House and contained gravel
floors set within a well-preserved timber framework. The size
of the structure and its Flavian-Trajanic date almost certainly
preclude it being civilian in character and the presumption
must be that it represents a large component in a military
complex, the nature and location of which remains unclear.
North of Tullie House at Annetwell Street several years of
excavation by Dorothy Charlesworth and re-excavation by
the Carlisle Archaeological Unit have revealed the exceptionally well preserved remains of a timber rampart and
military gateway (Fig. 27). It now seems fairly clear, however,
that the gateway formed the southern entrance to a fort
underlying the castle to the north rather than into a complex
to the south. In this context the position occupied by the castle
would offer an excellent strategic site for a fort of not more
than eight acres (3 ha.) placed so as to guard the Eden
crossing. The internal details of the excavated portion of the
gate, internal roads and timber buildings are amongst the
finest of their kind, thanks to the extraordinary degree of

Fig. 27   Military timberwork recently excavated at Carlisle

preservation of the wood. Detailed publication is awaited but through the courtesy of the Carlisle Archaeological Unit it is now possible to indicate the major chronological periods of the Annetwell Street site. The site was initially occupied as an Agricolan fort founded c. A.D. 78–9, a date that rests primarily on a large number of coins from the period A.D. 71–78 found in the associated levels. The structures at this stage comprised a turf and timber rampart, the gateway already mentioned, internal timber buildings and working and cooking areas. Within this primary fort some five or six sub-phases have been identified ending in large scale demolition (attested by bonfires) that took place very shortly after A.D. 100, again on the basis of numismatic evidence. After an uncertain interval in the early second century a second fort was built over the demolished remains. The internal structures were of timber and broadly speaking followed the overall layout of its predecessor. Once again multiple phases were identified which extended the life of the fort to a time in the late Antonine period when the whole site was again levelled. This development was evidently p-reparatory to the construction of a major stone building apparently of courtyard plan but in reality left in an unfinished state. It was overtaken c. A.D. 200 by the buildings of a presumed stone fort that partly adapted existing foundations of the earlier incomplete building. Within the excavated area two ranges of structure were investigated, one strongly resembling a barrack, with well mortared walls with roof tiles of sandstone and stamped *tegulae*. Amidst the considerable quantity of carved stones recovered was an altar of early third century date and dedication panels recording building by the 20th Legion. As one might expect of stone structures, occupation was prolonged, and it is difficult to ascribe a terminus to occupation within a broad period c. A.D. 275–325. Some slight traces of re-use were identified at an unspecified period and 9th–10th century Saxon crosses were recovered in much the same way that similar crosses have been discovered amongst rubble of the Roman site at Lancaster.

In overall terms, the later stages of the Annetwell site are difficult to analyse in the absence of the rampart and gate associated with the primary and secondary forts. On the other hand, the third century buildings with their legionary tile stamps must undoubtedly fall within a military context. In this case there might be an argument for seeing these developments at Carlisle as being parallel to the military compounds retained on the civilianised site at Corbridge near Hexham at a comparable period. The case for military occupation in the latter part of the second century is less strong in view of the unfinished nature of the remains, but the link in planning between the late second century and third century periods must also tilt the balance towards the probability of a military context at the northern ends of the town overlooking the River Eden. Further south, underneath the present city, the archaeologists are beginning to piece together elements of a complex jigsaw.

The historical picture must undoubtedly be a complicated one involving the rapid build-up and fluctuating occupation of troops at a major strategic centre throughout the period preceding the construction of Hadrian's Wall. It is worth noting that the massive Tullie House structure apparently lies on the same axis as the remains recently located at the Annetwell Street site, and may therefore belong in origin to an annexe or truncated version of the military base; the former explanation would fit in with the apparent absence of a ditch fronting the rampart, a situation paralleled at the Flavian fort of Strageath. On the other hand, given the topographical restrictions of river and marsh to north, west and east, some idea of the southern limits to military occupation can be gained from recent excavations near Blackfriars. A major road was located running south-eastwards away from the area of the Cathedral and St Cuthbert's church towards the English Gate. Along its western side a series of timber strip buildings was identified running backwards from the road. Although again of Flavian-Trajanic date, their small size and varying internal arrangements appears to preclude a military origin. They may therefore be taken as part of the early *vicus*, or civilian settlement, extending along the principal southern exit road from the fort or forts that commanded the spur overlooking the Eden (Fig. 28).

The way in which the timber and half-timbered building located near Blackfriars retained, broadly speaking, the same basic plans and building plots from the second to the fourth centuries suggests that the associated roadway remained one of the major elements in the plan of the presumably walled town and cantonal capital that emerged at Carlisle. Excavation in the area of redevelopment in the Lanes, the medieval core of the present city, shows that there similar structures, and a problematic early ditch, gave way to a substantial stone building in the late second/early third century. The lifespan of the latter was probably extensive but with limited evidence available from modern excavation it would be premature to make generalisations at this stage. Of historical importance on the Blackfriars site, however, was the replacement of the Roman layout by a large timber-framed building that obliterated one of the long-standing paved alleys, probably in the fifth century. This vital piece of evidence therefore provides an intriguing link with the situation mentioned by St Cuthbert in A.D. 685. The walls that he presumably saw were still those of the Roman town, doubtless partly refurbished by that stage. With the evidence from a site near Blackfriars it is now

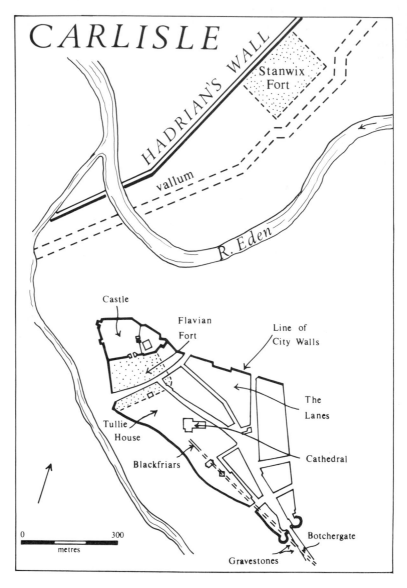

Fig. 28   A plan of Roman and Medieval Carlisle

possible to see that the line of the modern A6 marked by
Botchergate incorporated the Roman alignment through the
English Gate and so into the core of the Roman town. On the
other hand the Roman defences did not perhaps extend as far
south as their medieval successors. Roman cemeteries were
carefully placed outside the walls and in the last century a
large cemetery was apparently found beneath the present
Woolworths, north of the Gate. The great majority of the
cemetery material, however, derives from further south along
Botchergate proper and also from occasional fragments in-
coporated in the medieval West Walls. Botchergate was not
the only cemetery area. A handful of burials were noted in the
last century to the east along Warwick Road at Botcherby,
implying the likelihood of a road running along the southern
side of the Eden valley, possibly an eastern section of the
Stanegate now better identified to the west of Carlisle. In that
direction one isolated, but rightly renowned, example of a
tomb implies the presence of a western cemetery at Murrell
Hill nearly a kilometre south-west of the city centre. In 1878
workmen recovered the tombstone of a lady depicted as seated
in a chair with one arm over the shoulder of her son, the other
holding a fan and a bird in her lap.[11] Like examples from
Chester, South Shields and elsewhere the scene is framed
within a niche, in this case with a scalloped canopy surmounted by a sphinx and two lions. The unknown lady of
Murrell Hill joins Aurelia Senecita, Anicia Lucilia, Aurelia
Aureliana and the infant Vacia, all buried on, or nearby
Botchergate, to give us a glimpse of the women who came to
reside in Britain's northernmost cantonal capital.

The vici

Carlisle was the major settlement of the area in the Roman
period. There were, however, several other substantial settlements in the form of vici associated with auxiliary forts.
Unfortunately we know very little of the civilian arrangements
at Beckfoot or Maryport. Some forts apparently attracted very
little in the way of associated settlement. Caermote, for
instance, at the northern end of Bassenthwaite appears to
have no such settlement. This may, of course, reflect the

brevity of the fort's occupation. Alternatively it suggests that the fort's exposed position and relatively small size told against the development of the ancillary social and economic functions that are normally associated with the role of a *vicus*. This was clearly not the case at several other forts, such as Old Penrith and especially Old Carlisle, where the very extensive *vicus* grew to be larger than the parent fort. We must remember that even when continuous, the military occupation of a fort often fluctuated considerably in strength and that the civilian town provided the economic and social continuum. On the other hand the *ala Augusta* was stationed at Old Carlisle for an exceptional length of time and the size of the extensive *vicus* must be partly explained by the presence of 500 well-paid *equites alares*. The *vicus* was sufficiently large as to boast its own administrators headed by magistrates *(magistri vicanorum)*.[12]

Old Carlisle is important because it is now possible to see the fort and *vicus* in its broader context; what one might call an extended *vicus* has been traced for several kilometres around the fort area.[13] In this (Fig. 29) a number of farms can be seen to be connected directly with the *vicus* or indirectly through links with the axial Roman road. If we take the farms alongside the Wiza Beck and further north-east near Jenkin's Cross and Sandy Brow, then it can be demonstrated archaeologically that they were linked directly into the *vicus* road grid in the one instance and to the Roman road in the others. Implicit in this evidence is the presumption that they were tied both socially and economically to the life of the fort and *vicus* proper. Thus there is a rare and demonstrable link between town and country.

Moreover at Old Carlisle there is detailed evidence for the arrangements in the civilian settlement derived from both robber trenches of stone buildings still visible on the ground and from aerial survey that combines the evidence of the former with that of the crop marks evident in the periods of drought. These show that the *vicus* (Fig. 29) was principally laid out along the axis of the Carlisle-Papcastle road which runs clear of the modern main road in this sector. Fortunately, therefore, it is possible to plot out the core of the settlement along this axis. Link roads branch towards the southern and

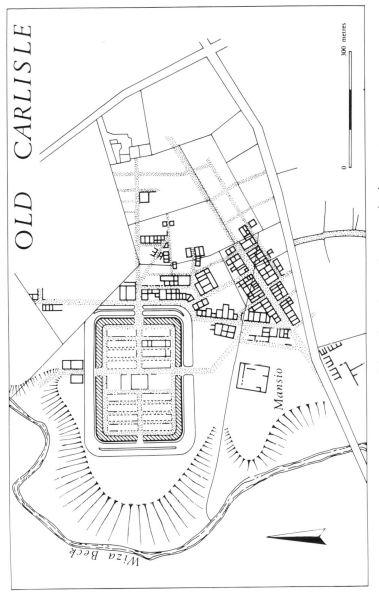

Fig. 29 Old Carlisle: a fort, vicus and communications centre

eastern gates of the actual fort and these too were flanked by
strip buildings. To the south a double-ditched trackway
springs at right-angles from the main road and runs through a
series of fields towards the large farm complex overlooking the
Wiza Beck. These small farming units form another example
of the field units recently observed from the air immediately to
the rear of the *vicus* of the Roman fort at Newton Kyme near
Tadcaster. Overall the dwelling houses, fields, roads and
lanes give us a picture of a settlement that exceeds in size some
of the towns known elsewhere in Roman Britain. What is
needed next is the establishment of a more precise picture of
the development involved and ultimately the chronological
relationship between the occupation of the fort and the *vicus*.
Contrary to what one might expect, these need not be the
same. At *Vindolanda* the extensive examination of the later *vicus*
has shown the civilian settlement was inhabited at several
periods when occupation in the fort is not attested.[14]

No other *vicus* appears to have reached the same size as that
at Old Carlisle. As we have seen, such features as the nature of
the garrison and its length of service naturally affected the
growth of each individual site. Other factors such as the
evolution of the frontier defensive system could also influence
the development of civilian sites. A newly-discovered example
is to be found at Nether Denton, the Stanegate fort in the
Irthing gorge. Recent aerial photography by the authors
showed that the earliest fort on the site occupied a far larger
area – about eight acres – than the fortlet previously known to
underlie the church.[15] The aerial reconnaissance also showed
the existence of an extensive civilian settlement south-west of
the forts (Fig. 30). This comprised a series of branch roads
running from the north side of the Stanegate. Building plots
line the minor roads and it is possible to work out further
sub-divisions in places. Nether Denton on the south side of the
Irthing was replaced in the Hadrianic frontier by Birdoswald
on the north. As is obvious to any visitor, however, the
northern scarp face severely restricted the development of any
civilian settlement at Birdoswald.[16] In the event, unless some
completely fresh evidence is still to emerge, it appears that the
vicus at Nether Denton continued in existence long after the
abandonment of the military presence. Certainly second

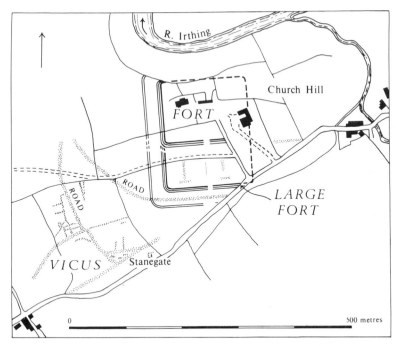

Fig. 30   The two-period military fort and *vicus* at Nether Denton

century pottery has been picked up in the *vicus* area to
demonstrate its continuity. There may even be a special
reason for this. Apart from Bewcastle to the north, the known
dedications to the god Cocidius are very heavily concentrated
in the Irthing valley. At this stage the possibility exists that
the civilian settlement at Nether Denton related to the *fanum
Cocidii*, or shrine of Cocidius, attested by an ancient source.[17]

The site that comes closest in size to Old Carlisle is the
civilian settlement around the fort of Old Penrith[18] on the
arterial road to Carlisle. Whatever the vicissitudes of the
military occupations involved at the fort proper, the simple
location of the site thus ensured that at the very least it must
have continued to act as a large posting station along the main
road to the north throughout the Roman period. The activities
of recent excavations there have, unfortunately, obscured still
further the remains of the *vicus*, on the size of which the

antiquarian Horsley commented in the eighteenth century. A whole series of buildings were until recently visible as shadow sites (from the traces of robber trenches) around the south-western corner of the fort. The recent excavations, while demonstrating that, like Vindolanda, an early fort or annexe lay under the later *vicus*, revealed several *vicus* buildings including one substantial stone structure that had survived into the fourth century and undergone several structural alterations.[19] The overall spread of the civilian township is perhaps the main point to emphasise, however, and it is clear from aerial reconnaissance that strip buildings lined the eastern side of the arterial road (now the modern A6) running alongside the fort. Behind them an area is known to have produced cremation vessels both last century and this, and so can confidently be described as the site of a cemetery. Behind this again on the initially gentle slopes running up to Lazonby Fell a number of farms and associated fields have been identified, although the picture is not nearly so extensive as at Old Carlisle.

South of Old Penrith the next auxiliary fort is that of Brougham, subsequently occupied in part by a medieval castle overlooking the crossing of the River Eamont.[20] For reasons that are not yet clear there are no remains of the *vicus* known to the south of the fort, most probably through the vicissitudes of modern agriculture. On the north side of the river, however, the picture is far fuller (Fig. 31). The Roman road ran north-west from the river to Frenchfield. The broad line of the road was defined by two widely-spaced ditches that were in turn linked to adjacent field systems. Lines of interrupted pit alignments evidently fulfilled the same function as the field ditches, not all of which obviously relate to the road alignment and may therefore be of earlier or later date. At least one site nucleus is visible amongst this material but there must be others adjacent to the causeway. Further away to the north, one is clearly located within a rectangular enclosure attached to a boundary ditch running half a kilometre north of the road. Close to this site a pair of ring ditches and grave-like marks indicate the presence of a cemetery of uncertain date. The principal burial zone in the Roman period lay east of the Eamont where rescue excavation

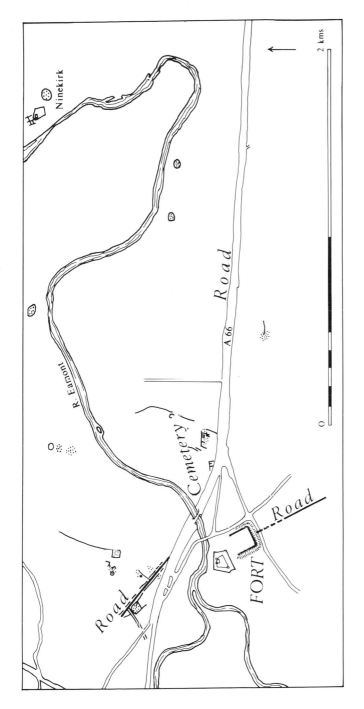

Fig. 31 Brougham: an 'extended vicus'

in advance of widening of the A66 trunk route revealed an extensive cemetery on the crest of a small hill. One of the cremation burials involved was surmounted by an imposing stone-built pedestal. Crop marks over the area suggest that either the cemetery was partitioned into several plots or that it was built over or overlaid by a field system.

These dispersed elements in the settlement arc around the northern side of Brougham merely serve to heighten the overall problem of interpreting the area. It is suggested elsewhere that the principal population focus of the area was the abnormally large site of Clifton Dykes south of Brougham (p. 7). The nature of the site and its size might suggest that it should be regarded as the cantonal capital (particularly when taken in conjunction with nodally placed henges of the earlier prehistoric period around the adjacent Eamont Bridge) and in turn explain the location of the Roman fort nearby. At present the scattered evidence for the settlement and agriculture north of the Eamont and Brougham offer an example of density intermediate between the well-developed *vici* such as Old Carlisle and settlement in the countryside proper. The evidence for the latter will be discussed separately in the folllowing chapter.

Shrines and settlements

So ends our review of the known civilian settlements of our area. It is important to emphasise that the list is an unusually short and restricted one; a major excavation in the environs of a fort, such as the *vicus* partly known from aerial photography at Maryport, could lend both greater precision and historical insight to the fragmented picture that has been painted. Yet at the same time it is worth emphasising that there were other non-agricultural settlements existing within this framework. We also know something by implication of the religious sites that formed an important aspect of the area (Fig. 4), which is exceptionally rich in religious dedications. Attention has already been drawn to the preponderant number of inscriptions relating to Belatucadrus recovered from the Brougham area (p. 10), and the existence of a shrine that they may imply. This is certainly the case in one other instance. The Ravenna

Cosmography attests the presence of the *Fanum Cocidii*, or shrine of Cocidius, in the area of the Wall. There is no doubt as to where dedications to Cocidius preponderate, namely the valley of the Irthing and the outlying fort to the north at Bewcastle. Indeed the latter has been suggested as the site of the shrine. While this remains perfectly possible, there is room for another candidate in the Irthing valley. The Nether Denton *vicus* (Fig. 30) has been described above (p. 62); its continued occupation beyond the lifespan of the Stanegate fort might also be explained if it was also a site of religious significance. Indeed various aspects of its layout known from aerial photography do not conform to the patterns normally recognisable in the plan of a civilian settlement. The argument is far from conclusive without direct proof from excavation but the possibility is worth stating.

Even more tentative must be our approach to another place with religious connotations, *locus Maponi*, the place of Maponus. Maponus was a native god often conflated with the classical Apollo, and the *locus* was situated, again according to the Ravenna Cosmography, north of the Wall. There are two clear candidates for the place involved. It has long been recognised that both Lochmaben near Dumfries and the Clochmabenstane near Gretna on the north side of the Solway contain the root *maben* (= *mapon*) referring to the name of the deity. On present evidence it is not possible to distinguish in favour of the claim of either site to be identified as *locus maponi*. What is clear from the other places listed in the Ravenna Cosmography is that *locus maponi* represented a recognised tribal hosting place outside direct Roman control but as such, formed part of the network of political surveillance amongst tribal areas north of the Wall. Clochmabenstane remained in use as a gathering place into the medieval period, but whether the kind of ephemeral activities involved could be recognisable archaeologically either there or at Lochmaben remains a matter for speculation.[21]

4

Rural Settlement

The type of settlement pattern and land-use typical of Carvetian territory in the Roman period was heavily conditioned by the environment. The tribal territory, like most of northern and western Britain, suffers from a shortage of lowlying, well drained and fertile land. Those areas that do exist have attracted heavy post-Roman ploughing and settlement. In these circumstances, almost all surface remains of Romano-British rural settlement within the more fertile areas have been destroyed, and the situation has been exacerbated by the current high proportion of this same land which has reverted to pasture. Under these conditions serious misconceptions concerning pre-Medieval settlement patterns have achieved widespread acceptance, not merely in the *civitas Carvetiorum*, but throughout highland Britain. It has commonly been assumed that farmers in the Roman period preferred the high fell slopes to valley situations, and explanations of this choice have varied widely – from the dangers of liver fluke to the presence of impenetrable forests. The assumption was based on the distribution of located evidence, which was dependent on the intensity of post-Roman land-use. Such an argument from negative evidence is invalid in principle. The achievement of aerial archaeologists over the last decade has been to demonstrate the practical invalidity of these assumptions, by demonstrating the widespread presence of rural settlements in the low-lying terrains of the tribal territories of the Pennines (Fig. 32). The impact of the environment is more complex than has been hitherto supposed, both in the rationalisation of the series of choices that confronted the Romano-British farmer, and in the ease with which the archaeologist can

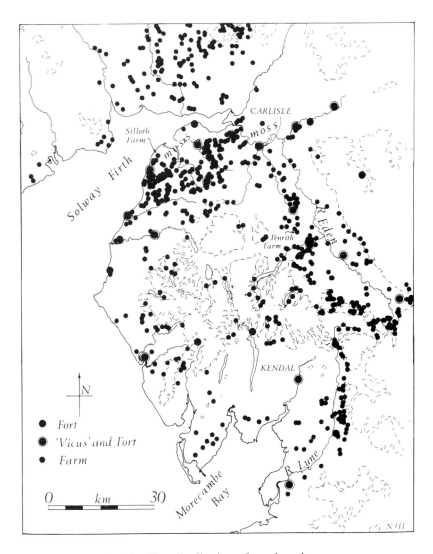

Fig. 32   The distribution of rural settlements

identify the material remains of the settlement sites that were located as a direct result of those choices. It is therefore, important to recognise that the tribal area can be divided, on environmental criteria, into six zones.

(i) The Solway Plain, and the Valleys of the Annan and Nith.

This represents the low-lying terrain on both sides of the Solway estuary where the land rarely rises above 30 m. The Solway Plain on the south side of the estuary is characterised by widespread areas of peat bog, locally known as mosses, which were more widespread in the Roman period. Interspersed with the bogs are sand and gravel eskers that rise sufficiently above the mosses to constitute 'dry' land. On the north side of the estuary, a relatively narrow but fertile and well drained coastal strip broadens out and penetrates inland up the major rivers. This area has an unusually high proportion of cultivated land, and is eminently suited to aerial reconnaissance.

(ii) The valleys of the Eden and Petteril.

South of the Solway, the twin rivers of the Eden and Petteril provide the obvious access route into north-west England. Their valley floors are far from flat, and contain a variety of soils. In the Central Eden Basin, around Penrith, lies the most substantial area of Grade Two Agricultural Land in north-west England. Even so, there are considerable tracts with acidic, poorly drained soils where late enclosure was the rule, and where agricultural land-use in the historic epoch has been difficult prior to deep ploughing. The largest such area is Inglewood Forest, but smaller waste areas are to be found, as at Musgrave, Soulby, Morland and Hoff.

(iii) The Western Coastal Plain.

On the west side of the Cumbrian Massif, stretching from Workington intermittently as far as Barrow and the Morecambe area, a narrow coastal plain provides a further low-lying belt suitable for settlement. Particular problems are associated with an assessment of the presence of rural sites in the area, because of relatively widespread industry in important locations along the coast, and therefore, although there has been recent fresh evidence of settlement, it is not dealt with in detail.

(iv) The lower Lune valley.

While it is not entirely clear whether or not the Lancaster area should be incorporated in *civitas Carvetiorum*, the fertile, agricultural lands of the Lune valley should at least be mentioned, even though the currently widespread pasture lands of the valley makes site location extremely difficult. Because of its uncertain relevance, this area is not discussed further in any detail.

(v) The upper valleys of the Eden and Lune.

Distinguished from the valley floors by geophysical factors, the higher reaches and valley sides of these rivers are typified by thin soils overlying limestone, treeless vistas and high pastures. This is the area where the most obvious, surface remains of Roman period rural settlement have been located.

(vi) The Central Lakeland Massif.

The greater part of this area is uninhabitable, mountainous terrain, of peat and acid soils overlying igneous or sedimentary rocks. The limited areas of low-lying terrain are either under water, or have been heavily utilised in the post-Roman period. The western slopes have exceptionally high rainfall, which further debilitates economic activity in the area. Although areas of settlement have been located, it is not dealt with here in any detail, with the exception of the Aughertree Fell enclosures.

While this is a schematic breakdown of the area into zones of environmental significance, it is important to remember the degree of local variation within each zone. The base geophysical factors are further complicated by the existence in the early historic period of several substantial forests, some of which may have been significant in the Roman period.

The Solway Plain and the valleys of the Annan and Nith

The Solway Plain and its attendent river valleys (including the Eden and Petteril) is the only extensive low ground within the *civitas*. Despite the presence of extensive mosses both north and south of the estuary, there is much valuable agricultural land. Until a programme of aerial reconnaissance began in 1974, only a scatter of sites were known in the Cumbrian littoral, and to the north, only those settlements still physically upstanding, occupying the peripheral rising ground above 150 m. Aerial reconnaissance, particularly in the drought years of 1975 and 1976, enabled approximately two hundred hitherto unknown sites to be located in north Cumbria.[1] The breakthrough north of the Solway came in 1976 and the two subsequent years. The pattern that is now established is one of intensive settlement of all terrains capable of sustaining a peasant population, with a concentration of sites on the lowlying workable soils, forming a dispersed but considerable exploitive system of farm units.

South of the Solway, settlement sites cluster on the small areas of 'dry' terrain – the sand and gravel ridges or eskers that are scattered among the mosses, rising often only 10–20 m. above them. A small esker might only have supported a single site, while more substantial ridges, like that on which Holme Abbey is situated may support several; in this case sixteen sites (and a further four probable sites) were located, all above the 15 m. contour, sharing an 'island' of 1550 acres (660 ha.), averaging 75–125 acres (30–50 ha.) to a site territory (Fig. 33). Evidence of field-systems is fragmentary, but considerable ditches appear to divide up this area into blocks of 15–25 acres (6–10 ha.), with most of the longer ditches running cross-ridge. Only a single system of small fields has been located, at Tarns, where ploughed out ditches delimit eight enclosures in all less than three acres. It seems likely that site location at Holme Abbey has been near complete, although none have yet been dated.

Elsewhere, a similar situation prevails along the east bank of the Wampool river, where a narrow arc of some 4000 acres (1600 ha.) not all of 'dry' land, produced evidence of twenty-two sites, some of which were associated with enclosure ditches dividing the 'dry' from neighbouring 'wet' soils. Similar, if lesser, settlement density was recorded elsewhere in the area, from Fingland ridge in the north to the Old Carlisle area in the south. As in all parts of the *civitas* territory, the

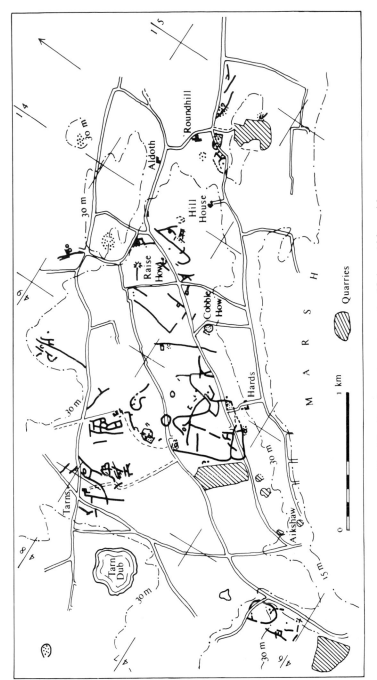

Fig. 33 Rural settlement on the Holme Abbey ridge

dispersed pattern of settlement prevails, although a few cases of paired sites have been recorded. Except, perhaps, at Wolsty Hall where trial excavation has demonstrated a rough contemporaneity, it is probable that here we are observing evidence for the re-use of a suitable location for a settlement nucleus, either after abandonment or after some disaster like fire had rendered the original site uninhabitable.

East and south of the mosses the terrain rises and clay and loam soils are less sensitive to aerial reconnaissance. Even here, large numbers of sites have been located, often in sufficient density to suggest a fully settled and exploited landscape. In the environs of the Old Carlisle fort such a scatter of sites is linked with the Roman road network, each other, and the *vicus* by a system of ditched trackways, in some parts coterminous with enclosures of agricultural type. Further south and east located sites are fewer, the terrain is higher and the soils heavier. In patches of fertile and mallable soil, sites are visible, such as the substantial twin sites at Sandy Brow, with their ditched enclosure system still visible under ripening crops over 10 acres (4 ha.). To the south no break in settlement occurs, but to the south-east, in the marches of the medieval woodland that formed the core of Inglewood Forest, a break appears to occur in the pattern of ancient settlement. Only in the vicinity of Carlisle and in the Irthing valley are sites present, but here specific problems – urban growth and permanent pasture on moisture retentive soils – have made site location haphazard and difficult.

North of the Solway systematic aerial survey in 1977–78, has identified about seventy hitherto unknown sites.[2] It was always likely that settlements would be found along the main arterial routes northwards via Birrens fort, and some of these sites are associated with the rare presence of field systems, suggesting intensive land-use, and perhaps, arable. A further example was located east of Annan. Elsewhere sites are mostly devoid of enclosure systems, and this is the case where the majority of settlements are concentrated in the Annan valley and along the broad shelf of fertile land between Annan and Dumfries. In all probability this population formed the core of the sept of the *Anavonienses* (from the river *Anava* = Annan) who underwent a census in the Trajanic period.[3]

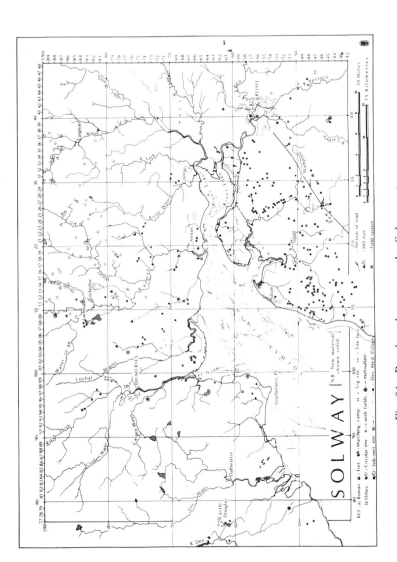

Fig. 34 Rural settlement on the Solway estuary

Major bivallate hill-forts were located north and northwest of Ruthwell and east of Dumfries (Fig. 34), comparable in size to Ward Law, and Torthorwald east of Dumfries. Which, if any, of these sites was the centre of the sept is unclear. The possibility exists that one of the religious centres – such as the Twelve Apostles stone circle or Lochmaben – provided the more important focus. Evidence for the latter comes from *locus Maponi*, listed in the Ravenna cosmography as the probable authorised assembly point of a tribe in treaty relations with Rome.[4]

West of Dumfries areas of high ground such as Criffell and the Stewartry uplands delimit and break-up areas suited to peasant settlement, and in the lowlying terrain substantial mosses, as in the Machars, and heavy clay soils limit arbitrarily the potential of aerial photography. Concentrations of new sites have been located on the well-drained gravels around Kirkbean, for example, where a trackway linked at least some of the farms. The majority lie on the seaboard and particularly

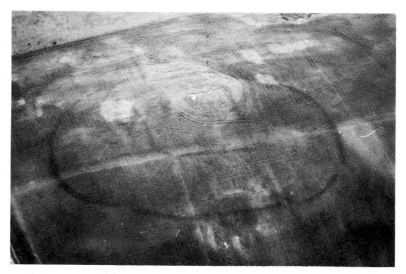

Fig. 35   Auchenhay, a two-phase 'native' site

around the estuaries, for example at Auchenhay (Fig. 35), where a two-phase hill-fort has been found, and Dundrennan, with several other sites along the Water of Fleet. North of Gatehouse a small trivallate site overlooking the river is more likely to be a civilian site than a Roman fortlet, as has been suggested.[5] A further scatter of sites has been seen, at Newton Stewart and along the shoreline of Wigtown Bay (South Balfern and Pouton), but elsewhere the 'wet' soils and current extent of pasture makes further discoveries unlikely at present.

Even though the programme of aerial reconnaissance has been only partially successful, it is at this stage valid to compare the pattern of settlement within different areas of the Solway lowlands. In comparative examination of settlement sites it is normal practice to make judgements based on a morphological interpretation of the layout of farmsteads.[6] While this approach is attractive and is to some extent unavoidable, it is arguable whether or not it has led to any real advance in the interpretation of the function, economy or date of a group of sites. The simplest type of morphological analysis – based on the division of sites into curvilinear and rectilinear groups – has already been offered for Westmorland, but neither the method nor the subsequent interpretation of a relative chronology of settlement have won acceptance.[7] If there is anything to be learned from a study of site morphology, it is more likely to relate to the function of an enclosure, and the land-use in the area immediately adjacent, than to the date of settlement. For example, it is noticeable that among the sites occupying the eskers west of the Wampool River there is a far greater proportion of sites of elliptical or curvilinear plan, as opposed to rectilinear, than have been observed east of the river. It is possible that this is associated with the relative scarcity of cultivable land among the marshes west of Wampool, where stock farming probably played a larger role in the rural economy than on the considerable tracts of cultivable land east of the river. A circular site incorporates the largest internal area within the shortest perimeter, and one should, therefore, expect an isolated settlement site to conform to a circular norm. The most obvious reason to abandon the elliptical site plan for new settlements is where the site is an integral element in an arable cultivation system in which a rectilinear pattern represents the optimum type of enclosure. No evidence of grain production was forthcoming when the total excavation of a rural settlement at Silloth was undertaken, but evidence of grain consumption, and therefore probably production, came from sites at Risehow and Wolstry Hall, the latter also on the west coast.[8]

In north Cumbria, settlement enclosures were in most cases single ditched and banked enclosures, normally with only one entrance, and rarely more than 1500 m.[2] in area. It has been suggested that such enclosures provided only slight security, capable of excluding wild animals. While it would clearly not be the function of the perimeter defences to withstand an organised group of armed men, they were probably sufficient to provide protection against thieves or rustlers. It is noticeable that those sites located closest to the Solway include those with the most considerable defences. The Silloth farm had a ditch and bank that equalled in area the enclosed space within, and a site equipped with multiple banks and ditches has been located near Kirkbampton.

If we take the located evidence of settlement sites on the south side of the Solway, and compare this with the body of evidence from north of the wall, some significant differences are visible (Fig. 36). Among the southern sites, 21 percent belong to an elliptical, univallate type, 18 percent are sub-rectangular, and only 11 percent are bivallate. Excluding the major areas of moss and tidal warp, 190 sites have been located in an area of approximately 700 sq. kms., that is a density of about 1 site per 3.6 sq. km. North of the Solway the terrain is roughly equivalent in the quality of land, yet there is a far lower density of settlement distribution. There were only 75 farmsteads located in an area of 790 sq. kms., that is, 1 site per 10.5 sq. km., and this in an area better adapted to aerial reconnaissance than is the case south of the Solway. Furthermore, sub-rectangular sites are less frequent in the north, most sites conforming to an elliptical, univallate norm, but there are far more bivallate or even multivallate sites. Field systems are almost totally absent away from Birrens fort and the Carlisle road. The tentative conclusion might be that sites beyond the Wall were thinner on the ground, more heavily defended, and less often associated with field systems or other evidence of intensive land-use. This might point to a major, local, socio-economic impact for the Wall, with a meaning beyond the simplistic version of its role to be found in the Life of Hadrian, *qui Romanos barbarosque divideret.*[9] The Wall probably hastened the development of a stable, agricultural com-

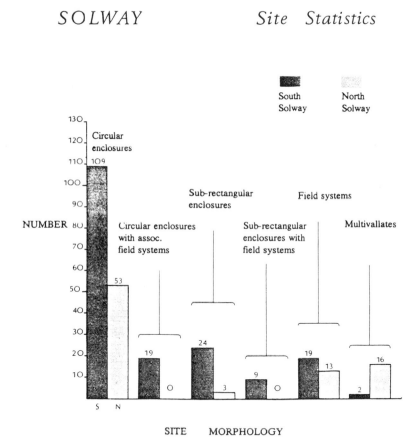

Fig. 36   A morphological analysis of rural settlements north and south south of the Solway

munity to the rear, and this development may be reflected in the differing site morphologies visible north and south of the Solway. Alternatively, the prevalence of defensive sites may reflect the insecurity off this small enclave in the pre-conquest period.

The valleys of the Eden and Petteril

The twin valleys of the Eden and Petteril rivers provide the obvious natural route from Carlisle towards Lancaster and York. With the exception of a handful of wooded areas and heavy clay soils, the area has been shown to have supported a widespread, and in some areas a dense pattern of rural settlement in the Roman period. Traces of sites located on the ground or from the air come from even the difficult terrains, such as the environs of modern Carlisle, and the presence of the two largest sites in Cumbria should come as no surprise. The bivallate scarp-top site at Dobcross Hall, Stockdalewath, seven acres (3 ha.) in area, dominates the presumably tree covered centre of Inglewood Forest where it is almost isolated from other known sites (Fig. 3). Pottery finds suggest occupation of the small central enclosure in the second century. The second site, at Clifton Dykes, in contrast, dominates the strategic and fertile central Eden basin, and it is in this vicinity that the largest number of new, valley-floor sites have been located. Until recent work in the area the poverty, and marginal nature, of site location in the Eden valley has been comparable to that in the Solway area. It can now be stated that the better agricultural soils around the fort sites of Old Penrith, Brougham and Kirkby Thore were occupied by at least a scatter of settlements, and it is likely that still only a small proportion have been located. The preferred sites are normally well drained, slightly elevated positions convenient for arable soils and water. The majority of sites approximate to a circular or square plan, with a single ditch and entrance. Bivallate sites do occur, as at Petterilgreen, but are a rarity. A number of sites can be seen to be associated with traces of ditch systems and even trackways, but only in a small proportion is a field system comprehensible. Substantial

systems are visible on unploughed marginal sites at Stone
Carr[10] and Blaze Fell, but the best example is at Yanwath
Woodhouse (Fig. 37), south of the Eamont river, within a 3
km. radius of Brougham fort in which a total of ten sites in all
have been located. Yanwath Woodhouse comprises an upstanding earthwork forming a subrectangular, heavily subdi-
vided enclosure.[11] Associated with it are seven rectangular
fields, and further boundaries traceable for 3 km. The field

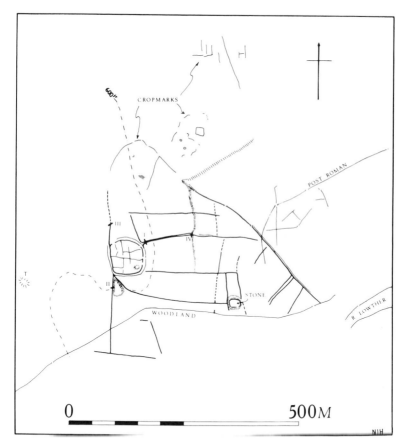

Fig. 37   The lowland field system at Yanwath Woodhouse

system has been tested by excavation, and been shown to consist of a network of stone 'walls', constructed from field clearance of stones, and ditches, with a well defined trackway. At least a part, and probably the whole, was in use during the second century. If this example can be taken as a reliable model, we should expect a dense pattern of dispersed sites in the area, practising enclosed, arable farming as well as widespread but only partially enclosed stock keeping.

The upper valleys of the Eden and Lune

Prior to 1975, the majority of rural sites known in Cumbria lay in the southern end of the Eden valley and its tributaries, and along the Eden–Lune watershed. It has since been possible to add significant numbers of new sites to those already known and recorded, but perhaps more important it has been possible to place these upland settlements in their correct context, forming as they do the upper limits of a settlement distribution that is essentially a valley and lowland based pattern. The accident of the survival of well preserved sites with their associated fields on the fells should not be allowed to influence interpretation of the total landscape to the detriment of the ploughed-out lowland areas.

The east side of the Eden Valley rises steeply and quickly to the exposed heights of the Pennine Chain on Crossfell and associated high ground. Medieval and early modern agriculture has obscured the terrain up to and occasionally above the 275 m. contour, and problems of site location are doubly compounded by the tiny proportion of this area which is currently under the plough in any one year. Even so, a scatter of isolated settlements have survived, normally occupying promontory sites on the banks of the swift, deep becks. A small number of sites have also been located high in the Pennine fells, above the villages of Long Marton and Murton, consisting of the foundations of undated stone-built settlements and associated irregular enclosures presumably intended for stock. A fragmentary but undated dyke system, apparently associated with two settlement sites has been located at Dufton, and it is likely that the fertile slopes of the river valley were widely occupied in the Roman period.

The situation is paralleled on the west side of the valley, in the shadow of the Cumbrian Massif. The slope up onto the high ground is generally steep, leaving little potential for the survival of early remains between the limits of post-Roman agricultural destruction and the high fells. Only where there are tracts of land between the 250–300 m. contours have sites survived as upstanding monuments. This is the case at Berrier Hill, near Greystoke, where a scatter of stone built sites has been located on poor fell pastures without any evidence for an associated field system. The settlement, with its field system, at Stone Carr has already been mentioned in another section. The field system consists of a series of substantial ditches that form irregular enclosures, but the whole has been severely affected by modern ploughing, and is now only visible discontinuously over an area 1500 × 300 m. Only two complete ditched enclosures are discernable, of two acres and one and a half acres. Their irregularity, and the absence of lynchets, means that these enclosures were unlikely to have been in arable use.

Undoubtedly the most important area of upland settlement in the *civitas* lies away from the igneous rocks and granites of the western slopes of the Eden valley, in the limestone and boulder clay terrains that are typical of the headwaters of the Eden and its tributaries, and the Eden–Lune watershed, comprising a band of high ground stretching from Shap Fell in the west, to Kirkby Stephen, Brough and Stainmore in the east. The most extensive, upstanding remains lie in the parishes of Waitby, Crosby Garrett, Ravenstonedale, Wharton and Hartley in the Kirkby Stephen area, in the drainage catchment of the Belah on Stainmore, and of the Lyvennet Beck between Crosby Ravensworth and Sunbiggin.

In the Waitby area, recent survey work and trial excavation have provided a useful addition to the published work of the Royal Commission for Historical Monuments,[12] and have made possible a reappraisal of the sites and their environment. The most complete complex of settlement and fields has long been in part recorded, lying on Crosby Garret Fell and in Ravenstonedale Deer Park. On Crosby Garrett Fell (Fig. 38), three extant sites and associated field systems occupy a plateau of limestone and boulder clay 270–300 m. high, above

Fig. 38   The upland field system at Crosby Garrett

the Scandal Beck.[13] Modern ploughing has encroached upon this plateau from the north, and has eradicated most of the early field system north of the central site of the three. The surviving field system is unusual for a complex at this altitude in being heavily lynchetted, suggesting the repeated use of these enclosures for arable cultivation. The terrain the three sites occupy is contained by natural boundaries on three sides – the Scandal Beck, the Severals Gill, and high fell terrain to the west, where an earth dyke which may be contemporary delimits the area reserved for intensive land-use, and may have acted as a barrier for livestock grazing on the fell.

In Ravenstonedale Deer Park to the south, the exclusion of early post-medieval and modern ploughing in an area of less marginal terrain has allowed the atypical survival of a group of sites with associated earth dykes.[14] Like the Crosby Garrett examples, and most of the other sites in this area, the settlements are enclosed with stone walls, sometimes of orthostatic construction, and contain both stone-built round huts, and in some cases rectangular or bow-shaped structures comparable to the timber-built rectilinear building style to be found in the lowland areas. The general shape of settlement enclosures varies considerably throughout the area, but with a tendency to conform to a circular or square standard. There seems no more reason than in the lowland examples to think that the shape of a settlement enclosure is of any assistance in determining its date.

The dykes of the Ravenstonedale complex are relatively typical of these features throughout the area. They are earth built, generally lacking any significant quantity of stone, and may stand anything up to a metre high and six metres broad. In most cases dykes were constructed along contours, and in such a way as to rationalise them, providing a barrier between open grazing and land used more intensively. In some instances a tenurial significance is probable. In many cases, a shallow depression is visible running parallel to the bank, normally along the uphill side. This has been interpreted as a ditch, and may, in fact, in some cases have been one, but where the method of construction has been tested, the bank appears to have been built of turf, and the depression was caused by the removal of turf for this purpose. While turf or earth walls are very little used for field enclosures, they were used a great deal in the medieval and early modern periods in the north, and are still seen in the Isle of Man.

Throughout the area, settlement sites are almost exclusively located on limestone, and yet never more than 200 m. from clay soils. Clay loams form the preferred cultivation soil of the medieval and modern periods. There is no reason to think this preference was otherwise in the Roman period, with only marginal extensions of cultivation onto the thin limestone soils, as occurred on Crosby Garrett Fell.

The Ravenstonedale complex is divided from the extensive remains at Waitby by a considerable area of high ground, which is currently in use as rough grazing and is devoid of early settlement remains. The Waitby settlements are separated from this fell by a considerable and complex dyke system, traces of which can be detected over 5.5 km. from Soulby to Wharton.[15] From internal evidence, it is fairly clear that the system is not a single, contemporary phenomenon, but contains a series of alterations digressing from an original, linear, barrier system (Fig. 39). The entire complex spreads across several townships, and may be contemporary with the other pre-medieval remains in the area. Uphill from, or outside of, the dykes lies fell pasture on thin limestone soils. The dykes provide a rationalisation of the 174 m. contour. Downhill from, or within the dykes on the valley slopes, clay soils predominate, and it is within this area that medieval and modern settlement has concentrated. Within the dykes, the use of a ley farming system in the post-Roman period has meant that few areas have escaped cultivation, even though only a very small proportion of the land surface is under the plough in any one year. In these circumstances, pre-medieval site location in the better terrains of the Upper Eden valley is near impossible, and only those areas within the dykes, but marginal to tracts bearing the marks of later ploughing, can be expected to preserve upstanding monuments of the Roman period. This means that the evidence for land-use prior to the medieval period is inevitably weighted to the detriment of the cultivation areas preferred in the later periods, and probably in use in the Roman period. In the circumstances, it is important that there has been trial excavation on the site

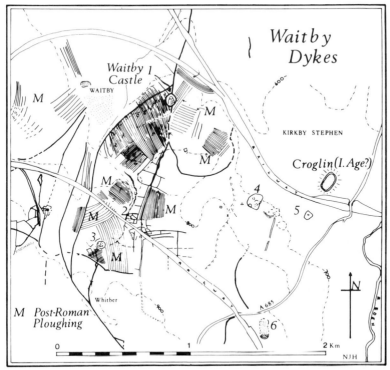

Fig. 39   The likely development of the Waitby dyke system

apparently associated with the exploitation of the Castle Hill fields.

The Castle Hill settlement site is situated on the apex of Castle Hill in a defensible position, 236 m. above O.D. on the parish boundary between Waitby and Kirkby Stephen. Its situation, and the surviving stone foundations, have given rise to the tradition of a medieval fortification on the site, but excavation has demonstrated the Roman date of its occupation. The earliest phase of occupation that has been distinguished, probably associated with the agricultural terraces on the western slope of the hill, belongs in the second century A.D. when the site may have been fenced, and was probably ditched. Cobbled yards occupied at least a part of the interior.

Either in the second half of the second century, or in the first half of the third, the perimeter was redefined by a dry stone wall, built on a prepared cobble foundation platform instead of footings. The outer ditch was abandoned, and an outer bank was constructed which considerably enlarged the enclosure. This phase seems to have post-dated the abandonment of the lynchetted field system on the western slope.

The relationship between the dykes and this arable field system is an important one, although neither has so far been objectively dated. From internal evidence, it seems likely that the earliest identifiable part of the Waitby dyke system included the sections on Smardale Fell and the short section in Waitby Intake. The remaining sections of the dyke seem to represent alterations to this line, in most cases successive contractions of the protected, lowland area in favour of the fell.

This progressive abandonment of the higher slopes represents a contraction of the area available for cultivation in the summer, and for winter pasture, since the dykes would seem to be the boundaries between areas of un-enclosed, or at least un-walled, 'celtic' type fields, and areas where open pasturing was simultaneously practised.

The association of dykes and enclosed trackways is also an important feature. On Crosby Garrett Fell and in Waitby Intake stone walled trackways connect the settlement sites with enclosed pasture within the dykes, providing protected access to the settlements through the arable-type fields. The presence of these trackways and the direction they take suggest the need to contain movement, presumably of herds, and it seems likely that such constraint was related to the existence of arable fields or hay meadows in the immediate vicinity of these, and probably other settlements.

If this interpretation is correct, the inference is that the upland slopes were under considerable pressure from cultivators and mixed farmers, probably most of all in the second century, with cultivation going on as high as 305 m. where soil conditions allowed, and settlement up to 290 m. When the primary ditch at Waitby Castle was filled, bones of the horse, ox, sheep and red deer were among the refuse deposited, suggesting a mixed economy exploiting an only partially wooded environment. With successive contractions of the protected area, we must assume an abandonment of marginal or deteriorating land that appears to have been both considerable and permanent.

The construction and maintenance of the dyke systems represents an achievement that must have been a communal one, however organised, since their proper functioning must have been essential to the economies of several sites. It is possible that we can distinguish a split developing in the community when the Smardale Fell dykes were abandoned. Earthworks are extant close to Smardale Hall that suggest a new phase of the dykes in this area, protecting the arable lands of northern Smardale and Soulby, while the last phase of dyke construction at Waitby Castle Hill implies an abandonment of the whole Scandal Beck drainage basin in favour of communities in the vicinity of Kirkby Stephen and Wharton.

These developments may have been to some extent caused by a drop in population, but there can be little doubt that the process was at least in part due to the detrimental environmental effects of over-exploitation of the upland zone. In the Lake District an enormous increase in fell pasture and bog plants has been dated palaeobotanically to the later first millennium A.D. but the physical evidence of abandonment suggests the process may have begun at an earlier date. It is unlikely that suitable, unexploited land was available to accommodate any surplus population in the lower lying areas, so that the archaeological record provides evidence of a society undergoing a retrenchment that may have been of significant scale and may have been as much self-inflicted as due to climatic change.

Parallel associations between settlement sites and dykes have been observed at Hartley, where a fell dyke rationalises the 335 m. contour and encloses the maximum area of boulder clay, being exploited by a group of settlement sites of which four examples have been located, along with a further possible five.[16] The Hartley sites may well be only the recoverable fringe of a considerable 'territory' to which the fell dyke provided an adequate boundary on the south-east. The Red Gate Gill drains into the Eden, so that such a territory might have stretched over much of the parishes of Winton and Hartley, and been shared by a group of sites with a joint interest in, and responsibility for, the upkeep of the dyke. The use of natural features as boundaries would be in keeping with land allotment on Crosby Garrett Fell, and within the Waitby and Wharton systems, and it is a feature typical of the Stainmore dyke system.[17]

A fuller picture of Roman period rural settlement has been forthcoming in the Vale of the Lyvennet Beck in Crosby Ravensworth where much of the earliest work on this type of evidence in Cumbria took place.[18] A considerable number of settlement sites are extant on the lower slopes of the fells and rough grazing at the head of the valley. Medieval and post-medieval ploughing has destroyed any sites that may have existed in the valley floor, except within the medieval deer park which has preserved the settlement site of Burwens, and the field system and dykes that appear to be associated with it. A recent survey of the whole area has enabled the compilation of a plan with all the early landscape features that are still visible, from the ground and from the air.[19] The settlement sites of this area are unusually large, and not clearly enclosed, stone built complexes with numerous annexes, some of which may have been used for hand cultivation and some for stock. Hut circles can be seen in many instances and are also stone founded, with anything up to six huts on a site. Rectilinear building foundations have been discovered on three sites in the area, including Ewe Close, a site which was partially excavated at the beginning of the century.[20]

Little settlement has been located in the upper reaches of the Lune valley to the north of the gorge at Tebay, where the Lune flows through a narrow valley between the fells of Langdale and Whinfell. Exceptions are all close to the river as at Wath, near Newbiggin, where a small field system and a trackway are associated with a small settlement. However, the majority of the located sites of the Lune valley lie south of Tebay. Two sites have been found in the southern entrance to the gorge, at Carlingill close to the fort of Low Barrow Bridge, and these are the most northerly in a line of settlements located along the valley side between 150 m. and 300 m. O.D., on average occurring one every kilometre down the valley from Howgill to Ireby. Few sites have so far been located west of the line of the Roman road with the exception of two sites near Underley Grange in park land, and a scatter of sites in the Kitridding–Mansergh area to the west of the Lune. The general lack of evidence for sites in the valley floor may be due to the greater intensity of later cultivation in the lower lying areas. The whole of the Lune valley north of Tunstall is currently pastureland.

The settlements in this area in most cases comprise single enclosures defined by a ditch and bank, or, where ready supplies of building stone are available, by stone walls. Where field systems are associated with sites, these are almost invariably constructed of stone and in most cases are also rectilinear in layout. However, most sites appear to be isolated from any field remains, although again this may be due to later destruction. Some of the settlements, as at Kitridding, are abnormally large, and hut circles – in most cases stone-built – are obvious in many cases. An exception to the univallate norm is the defensively situated, multivallate site at Leck Castle, for which a late prehistoric date is likely.[21]

While sites that are associated with field banks are the exception rather than the rule, those that are present are particularly important. Fragmentary evidence of enclosure systems has been located in the vicinity of several sites, but by far the most complete, extant, Romano-British landscape lies around Eller Beck, on High Park east of Casterton on an area of rough grazing land at 150 m.–230 m. above O.D. The system was first recorded in the early 1960's, and the results of a trial excavation of one of the settlement sites place the site, and presumably the field system, in a Roman context.[22] Recent aerial and field reconnaissance has identified many of the nearest, neighbouring sites, and recorded the field system over a far greater extent, which is now thought to encompass at least 60 ha. (145 acres approximately) in association with eight settlement sites and several trackways (Fig. 40). On the valley side, the original extent of the field system has been obscured by later cultivation. On the lower slopes where evidence has survived, a rectilinear field system predominates, with considerable banks and stone 'walls' running cross-

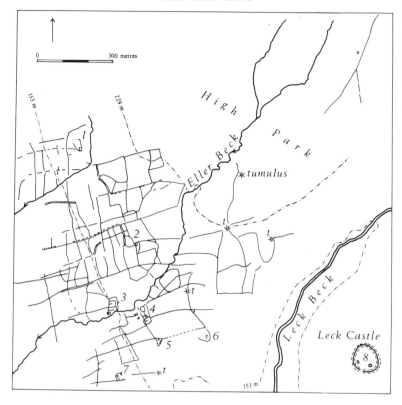

Fig. 40   The Eller Beck field complex in the Lune Valley

contour, and connected by slighter banks which are in some cases lynchetted. The whole system to some extent resembles a series of ladders. Above about 190 m., enclosures tend to be less regular in shape, and larger. Five tumuli have also been recorded from the area. The entire surviving sytem suggests a group of settlements scattered among fields laid out to a design suitable for agriculture, which are protected by pastoral enclosures from the un-enclosed summer grazing on High Park and Casterton Fell. The nearest local comparable systems are probably the field system on the apex of Crosby Ravensworth Fell, and the dyke system and sites on Aughertree Fell on the north side of the Lakeland Massif. The complex also bears comparison with the Grassington field system. The population of such a complex would be practicing mixed agriculture, and the surplus production may, as Lowndes suggested, have been destined to provision the garrison that temporarily made it worthwhile to extend the production of grain to these marginal terrains.

There is one further, important aspect of the Eller Beck field system that has only emerged from recent survey work. In two areas it can be shown from field evidence that there has been a super-imposition of an irregular, paddock-like enclosure, onto the rectilinear field system that dominates the area. One of these two later enclosures is apparently associated with one of the settlement sites, and it seems likely that we have here a further piece of evidence suggesting a decline in the area normally given over to cultivation, – at its height perhaps as early as the second century – and a tendency for the abandonment of marginal agricultural land in favour of pastoral use during the second half of the Roman period, a theory that has already been proposed on the basis of the Waitby evidence.[23]

The Central Lakeland Massif

The central lakeland mountains constitute an upland zone with few advantages to offer a rural community. Most of the area is high ground, covered by moorland vegetation and peat deposits, and the high rainfall and general inhospitality means that settlement has been restricted largely to the sides of the narrow valleys and the lakesides. The most complete example of a settlement complex in this area lies on Aughertree Fell south of Wigton.[24] The present ground cover is rough grazing, with coarse plants surviving in conditions of poor drainage on acid soils. Three clearly defined sites, a further possible example, and an extensive field system occupy the north facing slopes of the fell (Fig. 41). A further site has been located underlying late rig and furrow close to Uldale on the southern periphery of the complex. The field system is traceable over 1.4 km.[2] and is limited by later ploughing on all the down-slope sides. In certain areas, soil wash and quarrying have caused localised destruction, particularly in the immediate vicinity of the settlement nuclei, where it is possi-

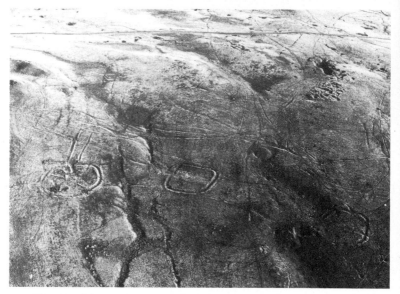

Fig. 41   The settlements and fieldcomplex on Aughertree Fell

ble that erosion has been accelerated by intensive land use during the life of the sites. Outside this area, the enclosures are considerable – up to twelve acres (2.5 ha.) – and irregular in shape, with the banks following lines which are dictated by the terrain rather than by any pre-formed notions, and were almost certainly intended to act as enclosed pastures. The best preserved site is associated with a 15 m. wide, banked and ditched droveway traceable for 300 m. running through the irregular enclosures towards the fell, and probably used for the movement of livestock.

Each of the settlements is defined by a deep ditch, with an inner bank and also a certain amount of upcast on the outer edge. Where internal details can be seen, there are banks dividing the sites radially into a number of compounds. The site at Uldale is the only one of these which is rectilinear in plan, but like the example discussed above it had a stone-built, round house.

Other sites have been located on the northern fringe of the lakeland mountains, but no comparable extensive complex has survived. Settlements have been located scattered over the whole area demonstrating the extensive nature of settlement in this difficult terrain.[25] On lower lying land at Eweclose, Plumbland, a well defined banked settlement enclosure is extant, and is adjacent to a small, terraced, plot system on a north facing slope, containing evidence of several hut circles and probably constructed to assist in small scale agriculture.

The settlements

Despite the recent upsurge of site location, there has been comparatively little excavation on rural settlements in the *civitas*. Following Collingwood's pioneering work at the beginning of the century,[26] only a handful of trial excavations had been undertaken before the seventies, – at Eller Beck,[27] Waitby,[28] and in the Solway area.[29] The most sigificant series of excavations was that conducted on sites in the Solway area, but these only served to demonstrate the lack of uniformity in site construction, and the date of occupation. Since 1975, further trial excavations have been undertaken, but only 2 sites – the Penrith farm (at Crossfield Farm 1.5 km. north of the town) and at Silloth, have been subjected to anything like total excavation (Fig. 42). These excavations provided only an inadequate guide which may in important respects be atypical of the majority of the sample. However, several point can be made, if only so that they can be reconsidered at a later date.[30]

Settlement sites normally comprise enclosed yards, huts or houses, and roadways or yards. The standard method of enclosure is by a ditch and timber revetted bank, but at some lowland sites, such as Jacob's Gill and Risehow, dry stone walls have been constructed, more after the fashion of the upland areas. Only at Penrith has the slot for an outer as well as inner palisade been observed, although the Silloth site had been reinforced by clay along the outer edge of the enclosure ditch on the weakest side. Outer ditches vary from 3–6 m. wide, and 0.5–3 m. deep, with a rampart that may be anything up to 3 m. wide. At Penrith the rampart had been revetted with timber uprights set in stone-chocked post pits. A large proportion of the settlement interior was normally cobbled to provide a dry area for animal standing, roadways

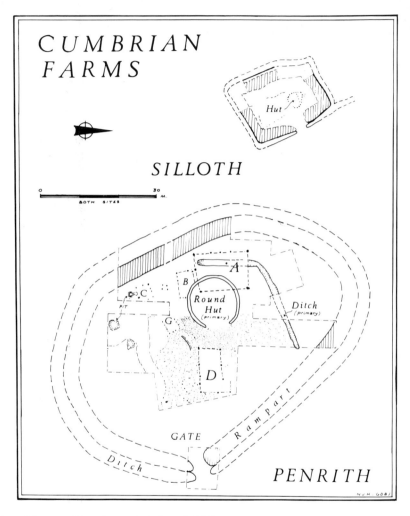

Fig. 42   Site plans of a) Crossfield Farm, Penrith and b) Silloth Farm

and work areas. The entrance is normally heavily cobbled and narrow – that at Penrith was about 3 m. wide – passing between substantial post pits in the butt ends of the rampart which probably supported a primitive gate. A narrow walk way passed between the ditch terminals, perhaps in some cases replaced by a plank bridge over a continuous ditch as at Brampton.

During the first half of the Roman period, the standard structure to be found on the settlement sites was the round house. In this respect, this area differs not at all from the ubiquitous Iron Age model to be found in Highland and Lowland Britain alike. The Penrith farm in the second century had a single round hut, with an outer ring of stake impressions and daub staining, with an inner ring of post holes for uprights providing the structural support for the roof. No evidence of a central upright was discovered in the closely cobbled floor surface, but there was evidence of fire. The diameter of the whole structure was c. 12.7 m. At Wolsty Hall, a similar hut measured 15 m. in diameter, whilst the third century round house at Silloth farm was a great deal smaller, with a diameter of only between 4–5 m.

A significant alteration in building style appears to have taken place in the mid-Roman period, probably during the third century, with the abandonment on some sites of the circular hut plan in favour of the construction of rectilinear buildings. Evidence for rectangular structures dating to the late third or fourth centuries has come from Old Brampton, Wolsty and Risehow, but the changeover is best illustrated by the example of the Penrith farm where the third and fourth century rectilinear farmhouse was sited immediately overlying the foundations of the primary phase round house. This rectilinear building, which retained evidence of a paved floor, was only one of four discernable, rectilinear structures on the site dating broadly to the fourth century. Although too few sites have been excavated for us to be able to make any specific claims, there does seem to have been general abandonment of the traditional round house as the preferred habitation, and this tendency is one that has been noted elsewhere in the Pennine area for the late Roman period, within the *civitas*, for example, at Dobcross Hall.[31]

The combination of new information from excavation and survey has provided us with little exact, or chronologically significant information, but it has produced a new general perspective on farming and rural settlement in the *civitas*. What has now become clear is that in most terrains not thoroughly waterlogged or above 300 m., there existed a dispersed and in some areas a dense settlement pattern of farm sites, associated with trackways, and to some extent with the Roman road system, practising mixed agriculture, some with a comparatively small, but still significant, bundle of enclosures designed for cultivation, and access to enclosed as well as unenclosed pasture. The farm sites are located on rational criteria which are rarely specifically associated with the Roman fort system, but dependent on the availability of land suitable for arable use, drainage, water, timber or stone for building, and fuel. The extent of enclosure systems, often visible in marginal terrain, suggests that for each generation substantial sections of the farming landscape were inherited. In other words, for many generations a high proportion of the important decisions had already been made; the system of land-use was predetermined and little change need have taken place. The important phases that must be examined in the future relate to the origins, and to the eventual destiny, of this system.

5

Industry and Economy

The vast majority of the civilian inhabitants of *civitas Carvetiorum* lived not in towns or *vici* but in scattered communities that rarely comprised more than a single family group. These groups were directly dependent on their own exploitation of rural resources, and were responsible for the provision of primary products for their own maintenance and, to some extent, that of the remainder of the community. The settlement sites these groups occupied have all the appearance of being scattered at random over the landscape, avoiding only the least hospitable terrains. However, the location of each site was once a conscious decision made within the framework of a set of tenurial or social limitations which we can only guess at, but with some concept of resource availability in mind. It has still not been possible to establish fully the lowland limits of settlement distribution, because of the prevalence of post-Roman ploughing and the ubiquity of modern pasture land. The upland margins of settlement are far easier to determine. Only a tiny minority of settlements occur above 400 m. and there is no certainty that the majority of these represent permanent habitations. In some parts of the tribal territory, the limits of settlement are significantly lower – for example, on the south and west sides of the Cumbrian mountains, no sites have been located more than 250 m. above O.D. The tendency appears to have been to avoid acid soils, on the granites and poorly drained boulder clays, and settlement reaches its highest limits on limestone fell areas where drainage is relatively good, soils alkaline, and pastures suitable for grazing. On low-lying terrain, settlement was most dense on available areas of easily drained sand or gravel soils, as on the Solway eskers. It is unlikely that such a dense occupation was present on the clays and loams that predominate in the valleys of the principle rivers, but aerial photography has at least demonstrated a consistent scatter of sites on such terrain, and it must be borne in mind that loam soils are far less susceptible to aerial observation than the freer draining sands and gravels. In the wetter areas of the valleys, sites are for the most part situated on bluffs and other elevated points where drainage is easiest. The pre-occupation of the farming population with the problem of draining settlement compounds was highlighted at the Penrith Farm where a drain of stone had been incorporated in the entrance-way cobbling to act as a soak-away for water collecting within the saucer-shaped enclosure.

Another obvious requirement for the Romano-British farmer was an adequate local supply of building materials. Within the tribal territory there are to be found two distinct traditions of house construction, one utilising only timber, and one using dry-stone walling for at least the dwarf walls of the house exterior. These different techniques appear to owe their distribution to the availability of building stone and/or timber. The stone building technique is predominant in those areas where plentiful supplies of suitable stone are readily available on the surface – particularly, in the uplands, those areas where limestone outcrops are common. It is unclear whether, in the Roman period, timber was a ubiquitously available resource. The presence of wide-flung signalling systems through the Eden valley are at least an indication that the area was not one of dense, continuous forest, and the density of settlement would suggest that the process of forest clearance was already well advanced by the second or third centuries. However, it is unlikely that scarcity of timber was often a problem for the rural population. Perhaps more revealing is the tendency for field systems also to be laid out with stone-built walls. This is not surprising in the limestone areas of the Upper Eden valley, where building stone was probably already a more economic resource than timber, but it is also true in some complexes where stone was far less readily available, as at Yanwath Woodhouse in the Central Eden Basin (Fig. 37).[1] The quantity of stone that was used in the cobbled surfaces of the settlement enclosure at the Penrith Farm is also surprising. The stones for these purposes may have been obtained from nearby stream and river beds, but most of it probably came from surface stone clearance of the arable fields in the immediate vicinity. Only in sites located on sands and gravels or on stone-free loams is stone not used in the construction and maintenance of farm sites.

To understand any further the factors conditioning the choices before the Romano-British farmer, it is helpful to turn to the more complete landscapes that have survived on the high valley slopes of the Eden and Lune valleys. On Crosby Garrett Fell, where three sites have been located, there is a super-abundance of two resources – rough pasture and build-ing stone.[2] Water is available within easy reach of most parts of the fell, and the presence of timber on the steep slopes of the Scandal Beck would seem more than a possibility. Locally, the resource that is most scarce is land suitable for cultivation, and the three settlements appear to have been sited with the intention of minimising the distance between the occupation sites and that part of the exploitation territory that was enclosed with small arable fields. No arable enclosures lie outside a 500 m. radius of the sites, and each is abutted by small arable plots. Elsewhere in the area, where sufficient evidence has escaped later plough destruction, a close associa-tion between site and arable enclosures is the norm. In some areas, like Waitby Intake, Hartley, and Eller Beck, the relationship is clear and obvious. In the valley floors less evidence is available, but supportive instances have been discovered, as at Yanwath Woodhouse and Thursby (Fig. 43). In the limestone areas, in almost every case, arable type enclosures are to be found on clay or loam soils, and are almost entirely absent from the thinner limestone soils. The high incidence of settlements on limestone, but within 100 m. of the limestone-clay interface, suggests a choice of site designed to facilitate the exploitation of a territory which offers a variety of resources, with arable concentrated on the loams – which have always provided the plough soils of the post-Roman era – and pasture on the easier draining but thin soils of the limestone.

The quantity of cultivation present in the Roman period in

Fig. 43   A lowland, rural settlement with its rectangular field system, near Thursby

this area has probably been seriously underestimated. Quern-stones have come from 'native' sites at Penrith, Crosby Ravensworth, Risehow and Wolsty Hall.[3] While quernstones are strictly evidence for grain consumption, rather than production, it would seem reasonable to suppose that a population regularly using grain products as food would have derived its supply from the near vicinity, wherever possible. Barley and oats would seem the most likely grain crops to be grown locally. Barley was among the foodstuffs named in the *Vindolanda* tablets,[4] and both were found in a Roman military context at Ambleside, while a single grain of barley came from a Roman context from the ditch of a 'farm' at Croftlands near Bassenthwaite.[5] Field systems that appear to have been designed with ploughing in mind have been found in too many locations for their presence to have been exotic. It is therefore arguable that the picture proposed by Piggott of an economy almost exclusively pastoral in nature (the Stanwick economy) as typical of the Northern British Iron Age is invalid for the Cumbrian lowlands in the Roman period.[6] The evidence suggests a rural population engaged in mixed farming, with significant quantities of grain being produced and cattle raised. While we should beware of over-emphasising local grain production, which was only one – and probably rarely the most important – element in a mixed economy, it does appear to have been a significant feature in Romano-British land use on suitable terrains throughout the highland zone. The evidence of the inter-relationship between barrier dykes and rectilinear field systems suggests a relatively intensive use of the landscape for both pastoral and arable production.[7]

The settlement site of Severals, on Crosby Garrett fell, is associated with an arable area of at least forty acres (16 ha.) (a figure derived from the calculation of the areas of the group of enclosures directly associated with the site as opposed to its neighbours, but excluding the eighteen acres of enclosures situated on the thin limestone soils of the natural terraces on the south side of the site as unsuitable for ploughing). There are reasons to think that some of the upland sites were associated with smaller areas of arable land, in particular where the only walled enclosures in the vicinity of the settlement consist of small, rectilinear, walled plots measured not in acres but in square yards. The best preserved 'plot' group is that in association with the site of Ewe Close, near Plumbland, but similar features are common at Crosby Ravensworth and elsewhere. In the more marginal site territories, the cultivation of only a few small plots may have been the norm, with the majority of agricultural production concentrated on less exposed terrains.

The evidence suggests significant differences between the land use in the better valley terrains and the hill farms of the upper valley slopes. In the former we should expect to find ploughing as a normal part of the farming year, with the production of a grain surplus. Where the evidence is forthcoming for the density of lowland settlements, the territory available for the 'average' farming unit varied from one hundred and fifty acres (60 ha.) per site, where rough grazing is available outside that area but adjacent to it, to five hundred acres (200 ha.) per site where no rough grazing zone devoid of sites is nearby. It seems unlikely that more than a minority of the hill farmers had access to a plough, but instead cultivated small plots intensively by hand. The widespread availability of rough grazing would suggest the raising of cattle, sheep and horses as the most important activities of these farms. The farmers exploiting the high valley slopes of the Upper Eden and Lune valleys probably occupied a halfway position between these two, with unusually widespread ploughing for terrains at this altitude possible only because of the effect of limestone on the soil, and a density of settlement which, if the terrain over 300 m. is excluded, is comparable to that of the richest lowland areas.

The potential food value of the annual harvest is difficult to assess. The small plots found in association with marginal sites may well have been cropped annually, with periodic application of farmyard manure for fertiliser. In this case, the areas of enclosed plots may have been a significant source of foodstuff for the farming community. On the more considerable arable systems, it is far less likely that annual cropping of the whole area can have been practicable. Given a primitive agricultural technology and a low rate of soil rejuvenation by the application of manure, a cropping cycle more frequent than once every three years is improbable, although there is no reason to think it as infrequent as has been suggested for the Iron Age in Scandinavia.[8]

The likely yield of food grain from the 'average' farm in this area can only be based on estimates of ancient grain yield per unit area, or as a return on seed corn, since storagepits were not a local feature. Suggested figures for yield have varied between 96 and 270 kg. per acre. If we take into account the yields achieved in the south of England in the medieval period, and adjust downwards to compensate for the shorter growing season in the north, a net figure of 116 kg. per acre (c. 6 bushels per acre) seems a reasonable optimum. Working at this order of productivity, the farmer at Severals on Crosby Garrett Fell might have expected an average consumption harvest from a third of his arable area of about 1214 kg. (1700 kg. minus 30% losses in threshing and storage). While many upland farms can never have produced a grain harvest in any way comparable to this, it is likely that valley farms had more, rather than less, land given over to agriculture than Severals.

The food production from the pastoral activities of 'native' farmers is even more difficult to quantify. Where there is any available evidence, cattle seem to have been the preferred livestock, both as a food animal on the northern fort sites, and on rural settlements.[9] Nevertheless, the bones of sheep, red deer and horse have all been found on rural sites, in circumstances consistent with their being used as food animals. The food value of cattle, per beast, is far greater than sheep, which was probably the second most common species, and it is arguable that cattle provided over 90% of meat consumed at Corbridge and Chesterholm forts.

An important factor in herding techniques in *civitas Carvetiorum* was the need to exploit the considerable areas of 'waste' land where no settlements existed. Such areas included the Solway mosses, and the high fell area that made up in all perhaps a third or more of the total land area of the *civitas*. The absence of sites from the area known in the medieval period as Inglewood Forest suggests that this was also an area of 'waste' in the Roman period. Exploitation of these areas was probably effected by a transhumance system similar in most respects to that operating widely in the medieval period, and the dyke systems that distinguish fell areas from those terrains where more intensive land use was taking place were probably, primarily, intended to serve as a barrier to the movement of herds from high summer pastures onto the valley floor. Although it is arguable that the summer pasturing of cattle and other domesticated animals led to the exploitation of wide tracts of unenclosed 'waste' land in the highland and the lowlands, the important factor that will have determined the maximum size of a herd within a site territory must have been the availability of winter fodder. This is particularly the case in an area prone to long, wet winters and a poor record of sunshine during the crucial haymaking months.

While it is both possible and normal under modern conditions to obtain a yield of hay of 1200 kg. per acre even as high as the 300 m. contour, it is unlikely that in the Roman period farmers could achieve more than a third of this amount. If we again look at the example of the Severals settlement on Crosby Farrett Fell, the area apparently associated with the site (within the Fell dyke and excluding arable and very steep slopes) is about one hundred and fifty acres (60 ha.). To maintain the condition of 200–250 kg. cattle under early modern conditions over the winter, a daily food supplement was normally provided in the order of 0.9–2 kg. of poor meadow grass, over a 6-month period. On this sort of calculation, the Severals enclosed pastures under optimum exploitation might have maintained a stock of 70–80 adult cattle over a winter, giving a ratio of one beast per two and a half acres of enclosed land – a ratio that seems inherently more likely than a recent Scandinavian suggestion of four beasts per acre.[10] A herd of this size, again under optimum conditions, could have provided a meat consumption yield of 3 mature beasts and 15 30-month beasts per year, providing something in the order of 2,100 kg. of beef – equivalent in calorific value to 12,600 kg. of grain. The combination of this estimate and that for arable production gives us an optimum consumption yield of 13–14,000 kg. grain equivalent for the farming unit. The addition of a further 20% for alternative food resources (milk, game, fish, etc.) provides a total optimum consumption yield of over 17,000 kg. grain equivalent. In practice, optima are rarely achieved, and it is probably reasonable to expect an average consuption yield of $\frac{1}{2}$–$\frac{2}{3}$ this amount. Given a per capita food requirement in a mixed farming economy of 750 kg. grain equivalent per annum (this is a high figure) production of this order of magnitude would have been able to feed 11–15 persons, which is a higher population than is normally thought to have been present on such a settlement. However, it is not unrealistic to suppose a loss of 50% of the total, ascertainable, net yield in the form of booty, rent, taxation or 'forced gifts', which would be the equivalent of the manorial and extra-manorial obligations among the medieval village population. What is very likely is that these farming units were capable of producing a surplus, and we should be prepared to acknowledge the importance of this surplus in the local economy, even if the vast bulk of it was absorbed by taxation.

Even so, it is likely that the food requirements of the Roman military garrison in the area imposed a considerable strain on the production economy. The soldiers' diet probably approximated more closely than the peasants to a minimum subsistence level (200–250 kg. grain equivalent per annum) since the calorie utilising processes, like the feeding of stock with grain, have already been taken into account. The figures offered by Polybius suggest a grain ration of 300–350 kg. per man.[11] It is clear that the military palate was provided with a considerable variety of foodstuffs – the *Vindolanda* tablets mention barley, vintage and sour wine, Celtic beer, fish cauce, pork fat, spice, goat's meat, salt, young pig, ham, corn, venison and flour.[12] It seems likely that the basic bulky ingredients would have been sought locally, if only because of the expense of carrying bulk products to the forts, many of which are land-locked (Fig. 44). A 500-man garrison would have required at least 163,800 kg. grain equivalent per annum. On a minimal estimation of garrison strength, for significant periods the Carvetian garrisons cannot be put below 9,000 men with an annual food requirement of 2,925 tonnes grain equivalent. It seems likely that the authorities were able to obtain a proportion of this from the area via taxation, and so avoid the prohibitive expense of overland transport, estimated at about 3.2 kg. per tonne per km. for grain.[13] On this reckoning the annual cost of provisioning Old Penrith from Carlisle with stores predominantly made up of grain would be

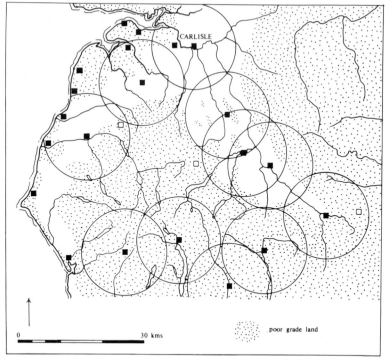

Fig. 44   The landlocked forts of northern Cumbria and their resource
territories

equivalent to 14 tonnes, and Brough 40–45 tonnes.

Given figures of this magnitude, the authorities may have
adopted at least two courses of action whereby they could
minimise transport costs. It is possible to isolate a tendency to
position forts on sites and in areas that not only conform to
simple military rationale, but also represented the choice of
sites central to areas of optimum production potential. This is
particularly true in the central Eden Basin, where the forts of
Old Penrith, Brougham and Kirkby Thore share an area with
an unusually substantial tract of fertile valley (classified as
Grade 2 land), within which they are unusually close together.
If we use as a rough guide the concept of a 10 km. radius
catchment area for fort provisioning, there are substantial
areas of the best quality terrains inside the catchment area of

two, and in some cases of three forts, while the poor quality hill country where bulk grain production was not undertaken lies outside. The location of forts at Carlisle, Old Carlisle, Brough and Low Borrow Bridge may exhibit the same resource consciousness in the original choice of sites. Even the route the Wall adopts between Bowness and Birdoswald follows a line that rationalises the distinction between marshland and the better drained, fertile terrain, and appears to incorporate in the decision-making process a desire to maximise the area of potential arable land within the frontier. It may be wrong to think of economic considerations initially influencing military decisions, but the eventual distribution of garrisons may owe something to these factors.

The second method adopted of avoiding exorbitant expense in fort provisioning was the use of cattle as a substitute for grain in the diet. Whatever the preferences of soldiers and the official policy, the delivery to forts of livestock on the hoof must have been a relatively cheap process, allowing the pastoral exploitation of quite distant terrain to be linked to the fort-based economy. The presence of cattle bones in large quantities on excavated forts in Scotland and Northern England would certainly tend to support this interpretation and, of course, leather, the most important by-product of beef cattle, was one of the most ubiquitously useful of resources to the Roman army. Cattle may have been driven to the forts from far distant, provincial producers, while it is possible that the army units involved themselves in food production within the *territoria* assigned to them.

The presence of nucleated civilian settlement outside at least a large minority (and probably a considerable majority) of the North Cumbrian forts introduces a further complication to the economic structure. It is still largely a matter of conjecture and supposition as to the basic function of a northern *vicus*, and the means of support of its inhabitants. It may be that a proportion of this population contributed by direct agricultural exploitation in the vicinity, as almost certainly occurred in the area of small rectangular fields and trackways adjacent to, and south of the *vicus* at Old Carlisle (p. 60). This type of activity, presumably linked to a military market for fresh foodstuffs, Celtic beer and so on, may have accounted for a part of this population. A further segment may have comprised absentee landlords absorbing a part of the surplus from rural estates, but, more important, there does seem to have been some economic inter-reaction between the *vici*, acting as centres of intra- and extra-provincial trade, and the rural settlements in their hinterland. The evidence for the presence of traders is to be found in inscriptions, for example probably that of *T. Aurelius Ateco* of third century date from Old Carlisle,[14] and there is no reason why we should associate such persons exclusively with military supplies. Evidence for local trade comes from the rural sites themselves, and comprises Roman type pottery from the south of the province and the continent, and bangles, metalwork, etc. which can only have reached the rural settlements as one half of a two-way trade. This would suggest that, at least on occasions, the rural population was marginally removed from a subsistence level of income, since imported pottery can in no sense be described as essential to the workings of the rural economy. A study of this inter-action is severely limited by the very small proportion of the sites that have been excavated or even sampled. Where sites have been totally, or near totally excavated, as was the case on the farm sites at Penrith and Silloth, the date of deposits vary from the early second to the fourth centuries. The total quantity of exotic material derived even from large scale excavations is small, and the bulk of it falls within the period A.D. 100–250, in some cases with a notable revival in the early to mid-fourth century. It is far more reasonable to argue that the phases of maximum deposition represent the period of optimum prosperity for the rural population and the economy as a whole, than to argue for site abandonment in the periods which are relatively or totally devoid of pottery. The absence of samian wares from the British market in the late second century certainly removes one of the dominant pottery types found earlier in the century.

There are a variety of possible explanations for the vicissitudes in the pottery record on rural sites, but other evidence is available from the study of field systems and settlement sites. From these sources, two factors emerge. One is the abandonment of agricultural land in favour of pasture and 'waste' that has been identified in the marginal terrains of the Upper Eden and Lune valleys, and the other, is the changing types of structure to be found on settlement sites. The agricultural type of 'Celtic' fields that have been observed at Waitby near Kirky Stephen, and at Eller Beck, incorporate evidence of abandonment, followed by new irregular lines of wall or 'dyke' construction that can only reasonably be interpreted as pastoral enclosures or barriers (Figs. 39, 40). In both areas these changes seem to have taken place within the occupation life of Romano-British settlements that have been dated by excavation, and that would appear to place the changeover in resource management in the second half of the Roman occupation. Two possible reasons for agricultural retrenchment of this type are a fall-off in the amount of grain being demanded locally, or a drop in productivity. On such marginal soils, the second interpretation is likely. With the numerical decline of the military establishment in the second half of the occupation, it is quite probable that the first was also a pertinent factor, leading to a renewed emphasis on livestock among the hill farmers and a decline in commercial contact between the rural population and the forts via taxation in grain and *vici* which had provided them with access to markets. Even so, it must be emphasised that rural communities attracted only small quantities of exotic material from the *vici*, and the exchange system was extremely limited. No economic development of great significance is visible in the Carvetian countryside.

The second factor – the development of new building styles – may have little to do with the relatively depressed economy of the second half of the occupation. A widespread phenomenon was the abandonment of the round house building tradition which had survived the Roman occupation, and the adoption of a rectilinear house plan in timber or stone. A group of such buildings, one with evidence of a paved floor, was present at Penrith Farm in the late third to mid-fourth century, and these represent the most sophisticated structures on rural settlements throughout the Roman period; comparable structures were found on settlements at Brampton and Wolsty (phase III).[15] This establishes that a building tradition indistinguishable from Anglo-Saxon building styles was present in a demonstrably late Roman context. Whether the presence of structures of this type are a gauge of the social status of the inhabitants is unclear, although there are numbers of sites, particularly on the fell sides where no rectangular structures have been located. Without a further extensive excavation programme it is possible to say no more.

It is hazardous to speculate on the total population figures during the period of the Roman occupation, or even during the probable population optimum in the second century. Manning has suggested a total population for Wales of 100,000–150,000 civilians in the second century, to which should be added 20,000 soldiers, representing a population increase of between 13% and 20%.[16] If there were over 9,000 soldiers in *civitas Carvetiorum*, on this sort of estimate we should expect a civilian population of 45,000–70,000 of whom 17,000–23,000 would be males capable of bearing arms. To approach the problem from a different view point, the total area required by a site territory was probably in the order of two hundred and fifty acres (100 ha.) inclusive of 'waste'. The Eden Valley and North Cumbeland Plain alone could have supported over 1,000 such territories, with a population nine or ten times greater. A realistic population estimate for the tribal territory at its peak may involve a figure of 20–30,000 persons, exclusive of the military.

In conclusion, the available evidence would suggest we are dealing with a substantial rural population occupying scattered sites in the 'dry' terrains of the valley floor and fell sides, engaged in mixed farming. Given the field complexes that survive, we should expect relatively widespread ploughing and cereal cultivation in the valleys even though evidence is still largely derived from tracts of marginal terrain at or near the 300 m. contour which have escaped later ploughing. Arable crops, however, only provided one element in the exploitation of rural resources, and pastoral farming was probably of greater overall importance in the economy. It is likely that arable production was very much geared to the needs of the military community in the second century, and tailed off, at least in marginal areas, in the second half of the occupation, when pastoralism became more dominant. While there does seem to have been some exchange of goods between rural settlements and the *vici* that probably provided the major local market situations, this is difficult to quantify and never reached significant proportions, or justified the survival of a *vicus* after a fort had been abandoned by the military. Even so, it is likely that a substantial rural population survived to the end of the Roman period, and there are signs of renewed prosperity in the changing building styles and exotic artifacts of the late third to mid-fourth century. The association between fort and rural population may have been sufficiently important to influence fort location, and in a few cases, farm siting, and it seems more than likely that there was a significant population in the area when the occupation took place, which increased from the second century, but may have declined to some extent in the later period.

Pottery production and supply

The pottery that the Flavian garrisons in the North brought with them belonged in style to a commonality of Roman military tradition. That is to say, pottery from the A.D. 70–80s found in Carlisle is closely comparable with similar material from other military sites across the country, and indeed on the Continent. Sub-regional differences do emerge when closer examination is made of fabrics partly, of course, controlled by the availability of local clays and the idiosyncracies of individual military potters. For instance, the carinated bowl with a reeded rim, like the pear-shaped jar so typical of the Flavian period, exhibits sub-regional variations in the use of the decoration between examples found in north-eastern Scotland, Central Scotland, the North-East and North-West. In the Carvetian area, as Gillam points out,[17] slight differences emerge between examples from Kirkby Thore, Carlisle and Brampton to show that production did not derive from a single centre, even within this relatively restricted area. Production was apparently on a highly localised basis; and Brampton is in fact the best example to cite because there an auxiliary tilery has been located close to the present town centre. The pottery at Brampton produced a broad range of tiles and ceramics including both a range of coarse wares, as well as larger mortaria, or mixing bowls, that share general characteristics with much Flavian material. Their distribution

on the other hand, appears to have been restricted to the
Stanegate fort at Old Church nearby. Carlisle, sixteen km. to
the west was supplied from another source.

The key to understanding Flavian-Trajanic pottery production lies therefore with the auxiliary pottery, normally producing both tiles and coarse wares, with fine wares being
imported from the Gallic samian kilns. Rather later than the
Brampton kilns was a less well known depot at Muncaster
supplying the garrisons at Ravenglass and Hardknott. Similarly, in the foothills east of Lancaster, the scattered production centre at Quernmore supplied both the coarse pottery
and the tiles of the principal garrison, the *ala Sebosiana*.
Potentially more important than any of these is Scalesceugh,
eight km. south of Carlisle, where stamped tiles of *legio IX
Hispana* known, of course, as the first garrison at York and
withdrawn from Britain during the A.D. 120s, have been
found together with some coarse pottery. Geophysical examination of the area has shown the presence of a large
number of kilns, which, if indeed associated with the brief
presence at Carlisle of part or all the ninth legion around
the turn of the first century, could be of the greatest interest
(p. 52).[18]

At this stage, while military production predominated,
some pottery continued to be imported into the region
through military contracts. The fine ware market lay in the
hands of the Gallic samian potters while roughcast beakers
were imported from potteries in the Rhineland. Amongst
wares produced in Britain *mortaria* production moved further
north; specialist potters operated at Wilderspool by the first
quarter of the second century and some from this group may
have moved their production further north to the Carlisle-
Brampton area, where their fabrics suggest that they used the
same clays as the military pottery.[19] This kind of development
was symptomatic of the change overtaking the market as the
military depots were run down or their work sub-contracted.
The change is most clearly shown by the advent of the
ubiquitous ware known as black-burnished. From the second
quarter of the second century to the middle of the fourth it was
the commonest kitchen ware in northern Britain. Moreover,
its introduction is a useful diagnostic in dating the develop-

ment of the northern frontier. Black-burnished ware (Category 1), now known to form a continuation of Durotrigan ware produced in the Wareham-Isle of Purbeck area and perhaps elsewhere, began to appear in small quantities on the sites of the Stanegate line. The speed with which it took over the coarse pottery market is shown by the way in which it rapidly became the predominant ware in the forts of Hadrian's Wall. Doubtless its sale was carried out by *negotiatores* securing army contracts, large and small. Indeed, one can see the patterns of distribution reflected in a number of wares. To take one example, Severn Valley ware appears to have been in circulation only on the western side of Hadrian's Wall, and only in the Hadrianic-early Antonine period.[20] By the middle of the second century black-burnished ware of Category 2 was introduced to the North but with an overwhelmingly eastern distribution reflecting seaborne transport from its production centre in the Colchester area. As time went on, production tended to be more and more concentrated in fewer and larger centres. The Hartshill-Mancetter *mortaria* kilns took over the lion's share of the later second century market and the Nene Valley potters developed the export of their specialised wares. Much must have depended on the commercial energy of the middle-men involved in promoting the sales of the later, minor types of pottery.

Relatively coarse Derbyshire wares were slow to develop but later varieties reached the north-western markets at Brampton and Bewcastle. Dales ware (in fact probably produced in Lincolnshire or Nottinghamshire) was another fabric that clearly expanded only with its potters' development of effective marketing, because it appears in its production area half a century before reaching the North. For whatever reason, however, the development of East Yorkshire wares was faster and Huntcliff and Crambeck wares dominated the late fourth century market in the North. Throughout this time, from the evidence of the very few excavated farm sites, a black coarse-gritted fabric assumed to be of local origin appeared in a broad range of contexts. It was assumed to be Iron Age in date by Blake, but there is no independent evidence to support this.[21] While in origin it may well be of pre-Roman date, it is now clear from both the Silloth and

Penrith farms that the fabric remained in production into the third and, in the latter case, fourth centuries. Significantly, it has yet to be identified on any of the early military sites, and this demonstrates the way in which the system of military supply could bypass, or in places overwhelm, locally produced wares of low quality. Nonetheless, the local native tradition on the present evidence survived at least in the rural areas through to the end of the Roman period. The pottery itself urgently needs heavy mineral analysis to identify its possible sources of production more closely, while identification and excavation of a partly, or wholly, pre-Roman site may yet give the Iron Age pedigree that Blake postulated.

Mining and Quarrying

The picture of mining and quarrying in north Cumbria is not by any means a complete one and we may expect a far fuller account to be possible in the future. The evidence for stone quarrying is widespread and not solely related to supplying Hadrian's Wall. East of the River Eden, the supply of good stone suitable for building is not as limited as is sometimes thought since sandstone, if not limestone, is available in several localities. Not so many quarries supplying the Wall are known west of the Irthing, but Coombe Crag overlooking the Irthing valley west of Birdoswald is as good an example as any, where it is possible to see the names left recorded by troops on quarry duties. Securus, Maternus Iulius and Stadus are all names to be found cut in the rock face, but the most interesting is Daminius, who left an inscription both memorable and to the point, saying that he did not want to do the work.[22]

A further example of a quarry used in the construction of the Wall is at Grinsdale, on the Eden west of Carlisle, but the other quarries relate perhaps less to the Wall proper than to associated sites. The quarry attested at Shawk, or Chalk, south-east of Dalston on the southern side of Carlisle, probably served Old Carlisle and its vicus with building stone. In fact a road leading in the direction of the quarry has been located by aerial photography in the environs of the fort (Fig. 11). The quarries alongside the Eden at Wetheral may have

supplied stone that was then transported downstream, to
Carlisle and even beyond. The best known site, however, lies
south of Brampton on the River Gelt. The 'Written Rock of
Gelt' comprises a series of names inscribed on the rock face of
a quarry cut alongside a tributary of the Irthing, and,
amongst the individual names, attests the presence of a
detachment from the second legion at work under their *optio*,
Agricola, in A.D. 207.[23]

Similar stone quarries are known along the banks of the
Crowdundle Beck, four km. north of the auxiliary fort at
Kirkby Thore. They lie very close to the line of the Maiden
Way, the dramatically engineered Roman road that climbed
north from Kirkby Thore across the shoulder of Alston Edge
towards the fort at Whitley Castle in the upper valley of the
South Tyne and then ran north to the strategically placed
Stanegate and Hadrianic fort at Carvoran (see p. 42). The
Crowdundle quarries may have supplied hard core for this
considerable engineering project, as well as building stone for
the fort.[24]

While the bulk of the local stone quarrying was destined for
military, and, to a much lesser extent, civilian building, it is
highly likely that the school of sculptors that has recently been
located in Carlisle (Fig. 45) were utilising local sources of
sandstone.[25] The school, the first to be positively identified in a
British centre, was operative at least from the Antonine period
until well into the third century. Products of this group have
been found predominantly in and around Carlisle itself –
including the finest example so far discovered, the Murrell
Hill gravestone of a woman and child (Fig. 46), – but finds
from Bowness and Old Carlisle also seem to be from this
centre, suggesting that the Carlisle school was both vigorous
and successful.

South from Kirkby Thore lay the fort at Brough-under-
Stainmore controlling the western approach to the pass.
Amongst the many casual finds exposed there by erosion were
numerous lead seals implying the presence of a centre for
collection and dispatch of some kind. Such an establishment
would probably have been under the control of a procurator's
agent and an intriguing Greek inscription found at Brough
church may record the death of the official's son, Hermes,

Fig. 45   Tombstone of Aurelia Aureliana, Carlisle (courtesy of E.J.
Phillips)

whose origin is given as Commagene; alternatively the dead
youth might simply have been the son of a trader from that
area.[26] But it is with the lead seals that we are principally
concerned and lead is the major mineral resource of the area
to the east along Alston Edge. There is unfortunately very
little firm evidence on which to estimate the extent of the
undoubted Roman involvement in its extraction.

Part of the reason for this uncertainty is that early modern
methods of hydraulic sluicing in particular on Alston Edge

Fig. 46   Tombstone from Murrell Hill, Carlisle (courtesy of E.J. Phillips)

differed little from methods developed, admittedly in a different mineralogical context, by the Romans notably in North-Western Spain and at Dolaucothi in south-west Wales.[27] Nor does the occurrence of simple bell-pits, or pitting as they are sometimes termed, give any indication of date. It seems clear, however, that Whitley Castle, the fort in the South Tyne valley, was concerned with mineral extraction as well as policing the strategic route from western Stainmore to Carvoran overlooking the Greenhead gap on the Wall (Fig. 8).

Indeed the extraordinary multiple defences at Whitley Castle
may imply the need to protect a strong room. The importance
of lead to the Romans lay in the need for silver bullion which
was extracted from it by the process of cupellation. Thus the
early silver-lead ingots from the Charterhouse mines found
near the Solent and in Northern France were almost certainly
in transit to a mint for further processing. Not that official
agencies were the only elements involved in metal processing.
A large collection of principally bronze objects intermittently
recovered from Brough-under-Stainmore,[28] suggests the presence of a local workshop in the upper Eden valley, either at
Brough or possibly Kirkby Thore. The metal concerned need
not cause surprise. Modern exploitation of Dun Fell and Cross
Fell, the highest part of Alston Edge evidently produced a
broad spectrum of minerals including both copper and silver,[29]
and the hydraulic remains still visible invite survey from
industrial archaeologists.

It is not yet possible to pick out detailed evidence for earlier
workings amid the very extensive remains that spread from
the source of the Tees and its highest tributaries across Alston
Moor to the Black Burn which flows into the South Tyne at
Alston. One can only indicate the likeliest areas for Roman
exploitation by extensive pitting. One of these lies close to
Whitley Castle proper. As the Maiden Way climbs away from
Gilderdale Burn to cross the ridge of Gilderdale Forest an
extensive area of pitting can best be appreciated from the air
and probably was the mining zone related to the fort. Further
south workings at the head of the Tees on Dun Fell and Cross
Fell would have been serviced from Kirkby Thore. Further
south again there is abundant evidence of early modern
exploitation on the south-eastern continuation of Alston Edge,
namely, Hilton, Burton and Warcop Fells running into Western Stainmore. Production in this area would have been
controlled from Brough-under-Stainmore; unfortunately the
presence of a military firing range makes it impossible to
survey much of the likeliest extraction areas but the proximity
of forts in the Upper Eden valley may in part be due to the
need to secure the production of silver lead and other minerals
from the wide variety of extraction points available along the
ridge of Alston Edge to the east.

6

The late Fourth and Fifth Centuries

By the third century the Roman provincial administration had changed: by the fourth century, perhaps abetted by the tide of regionalism, it had altered still further. The province of Britain was sub-divided into two provinces, *Britannia Inferior* and *Britannia Superior* under the emperor Severus or his son Caracalla. The precise date is disputed. One source, the writer Herodian, ascribes the move to precautionary measures after the defeat of Albinus, the British contender for the imperial throne, at the battle of Lugdunum in A.D. 197.[1] Herodian's statement raises problems about the presence side by side of a consular govenor, legate Alfenus Senecio, and the procurator Oclatinius Adventus on the Wall and the eastern outpost forts in the early years of the third century. Most discussions of the problem have tried to explain away these anomalies (on the earlier dating) as measures of temporary expediency. In an ingenious argument E. Birley suggested, on the basis of the Middleton milestone, that the procuratorial province of *Inferior* excluded York and the Sixth legion and instead had its capital at Carlisle amongst the Carvetii.[2] Most modern critics, however, are moving away from Herodian's statement towards a later date. In a new study A.R. Birley has pointed out the importance of a dedication made to the consul C. Iulius Asper in A.D. 212 which describes him as patron of *provincia Britannia*, i.e. a single province.[3] It currently seems possible that Herodian was confused by parallel events in the division of Syria and that the actual division took place after A.D. 212 under Caracalla. If so, then the setting for the move is comparable to that postulated after the Battle of Lugdunum, in this case the disaffection of Britain owing to Caracalla's murder of his brother Geta. The governor Iulius Marcus' protestations of loyalty on a series of dedications were of no avail and the erasure of his name attests the gravity of the sitation in Britain. This then is the likely context for the first sub-division.

It is possible that further sub-division may have occurred under the Gallic emperors (A.D. 260–74) but more probably the two provinces continued as the administrative arrangement until the succession of Carausius and Allectus (A.D. 287–296). By the time the Verona List was compiled between A.D. 312 and 314 there were four provinces known formally as the dioceses of Britain; they comprised *Prima*, *Secunda*, *Maxima Caesariensis* and *Flavia Caesariensis*. There is much dispute over two of these titles but not over *Secunda* which is generally agreed to be the new title for a somewhat altered *Britannia Inferior*, probably with the Humber as its southern boundary. Another northern province was created by A.D. 367–8 at the time of Theodosius' reconstruction in the wake of the great barbarian conspiracy. Despite ambivalences in the historian Ammianus Marcellinus' account, the *Notitia Dignitatum* (see p. 123) makes it clear that a newly designated area was involved, namely *Valentia*. It may be that the provincial zone already existed under another name, perhaps created by the emperor Constans on his special visit in the winter of A.D. 343 when *Secunda* may have been sub-divided. Certainly *Valentia* should be seen in the North, and perhaps the North-West, with Carlisle the obvious capital if that was the case. Whatever the answer, Ammianus' description makes it practically certain that the forts of the Wall lay in *Valentia*.[4] Our archaeological picture of the end of Roman control in the North-West must indeed begin with an understanding of the strategy involved in the army's grip on Hadrian's Wall, and the frontier zone.

The military situation

By the fourth century the nature of the Roman army had changed. While the existence of a permanent field army, the *comitatenses*, can be assumed, principally from analogy elsewhere, to have formed the military backbone of provincial defence, the nature of the auxiliary troops on the border had changed substantially, as had the rules of military service. This did not mean simply that from the third century soldiers were allowed to make recognised marriages; in addition, with the consequent reduced mobility of units, they lived and served in their forts – hence their name *limitanei*, 'the people of the frontier'. If we look at Housesteads with its possible cultivation terraces[5] we can see that in its later phases the fort was approaching the analogy of a fortified village set, perhaps, amongst strip fields on which it relied for much of its provisions (see further p. 126). Already, by the third century, at Housesteads, the nature of the military garrison was changing. The presence of the *cuneus Hnaudifridi*, Notfried's irregulars, attests that Germanic mercenary troops were being brought in from outside the Empire.[6] The irregular unit of Frisian Cavalry also attested about the same time at Housesteads is now known to have persisted with its own characteristic pottery forms when in garrison.[7]

In what circumstances was the Wall garrison of the later fourth century operating? We know its late dispositions from the *Notitia Dignitatum*, a late army list probably compiled in the first quarter of the fifth century when Britain was no longer formally under Roman control. Yet it is generally agreed that it contains a strand of information about Britain relating to the last quarter of the fourth century, probably before A.D. 383 when Magnus Maximus (the Maxsen Wledig of Welsh heroic poetry) perhaps stripped the country of its garrison to support his gamble for the imperial throne. The *Notitia* shows that the bulk of the Wall forts were still garrisoned and lists the garrisons concerned.[8] The two arterial routes from the south both appear to have been garrisoned though the emphasis is heavily on the eastern side where the military link was with York. Indeed, the principal, garrisoned approach to Carlisle from the south appears to have lain over the Stainmore Pass, emphasising the strategic importance of York. Significantly the line of occupied forts is shown continuing round the Cumbrian coast to Maryport, Burrow Walls, Moresby and further south still to Ravenglass. As if to emphasise the seaborne threat, Lancaster is also noted in the *Notitia* and was by this stage a coastal defence fort of the Saxon shore variety, founded in the A.D. 330s or very shortly after.

It was in the earlier years of the fourth century (the traditional Hadrian's Wall Period III) that the shape of the frontier took its final form. The work of restoration undertaken by Constantius Chlorus at the beginning of Period III can be said to have reconstituted the Wall as a defensive zone, whatever the arguments about the extent of the destruction that he had to face. The difficulty confronting historians and archaeologists lies in discerning the significant from the coincidentally surviving evidence in a period where the relevant books of its principal chronicler, Ammianus Marcellinus, are lost. This is one reason for re-emphasising the significance of the intervention by the emperor Constans in a worsening political situation in A.D. 343. The construction of the coastal fort at Lancaster (known as the Wery Wall), like that at Pevensey in the south, can now be ascribed to his reign on coin evidence.[9] This initiative reflects the growing threat of seaborne attacks across the Irish Sea. That it did not stand in isolation is shown by a cryptic reference to the *arcani*, the fourth century equivalent of the third century *exploratores* who were responsible for frontier surveillance in the outpost forts.[10] Constans reorganised this force in a way that is not understood but the new arrangements must have been the key to understanding the events of the A.D. 360s.

In that decade an army already depleted by Britain's disastrous support of Magnentius on the continent was incapable of withstanding attacks from a growing number of quarters. In A.D. 360 the new emperor Julian's *magister equitum*, Lupicinus, was sent to cope with the Picts of central Scotland and the Scots (still based in Ireland at this time) who had broken the existing treaty arrangements. He dealt with the situation quickly but the pause was brief. Attacks by the Picts, Scots, Saxons and Attacotti around A.D. 365 were but the prelude to the great 'barbarian conspiracy' of two years later when the Franks joined the Saxons in attacking the east coast while the weight of the Picts, Scots and Attacotti (either from Ireland or the Western Isles) fell upon the northern frontier and the North-West.[11]

Archaeologists have long discussed the extent and nature of the destruction inflicted in the A.D. 360s. In our area the bath-house at the outpost fort of Bewcastle was completely destroyed and never rebuilt, and at a few other forts actually on the Wall there is clear evidence of destruction; Rudchester, Haltonchesters, South Shields and possibly Wallsend were abandoned at the time. Despite problems of detail it is clear from Ammianus Marcellinus' account[12] that the Saxons, Picts, and the tribes from the Irish Sea succeeded in overwhelming the province from at least three sides resulting in the death of the Count of the Saxon Shore and the defeat, capture or siege of the commander in chief, the *dux Britanniarum*. The extent of the disaster was partly due to the treachery of the *arcani*,[13] previously mentioned. They sided with the enemy instead of performing their role as advance guards channelling information to the Roman military command. This estrangement of the very people whose surveillance was intended to protect the northern frontier was symptomatic of the changed nature of the frontier strategy. The *arcani* were but one part of the defence in depth that had supplanted the confident use of the Wall as a defensible, linear frontier in the second century. The disuse of forts, their varied occupation and the apparent neglect of turrets and some of the milecastles in the fourth century points the way in which the mural curtain proper was of decreasing importance in the overall pattern of defensive strategy. This rested on the creation of highly defended strongpoints capable of existing in isolation for some time until the arrival of the main field army. Opponents pushing south would find it difficult to reduce these defended strongpoints or gain the food supplies stored within them. When the initial push had been absorbed and the mobile field army begun the process of counter-attack, the remote strongpoints could deploy their forces to hinder or encircle the retreating enemy. Yet it is clear from the events of A.D. 367 that these developments were double-edged. The *arcani* in their outposts were likely to feel increasingly remote from the empire they were designed to forewarn, whilst developing sympathies with the potential enemy. The composition of the *arcani* is unfortunately not known but, if we remember the German mercenaries of the *cuneus Hnaudifridi*, that formed part of the third century garrison at Housesteads, it is easy to see how they would come to feel a greater affinity with tribal soldiers promising booty than with the late imperial command.[14]

Theodosius was specially dispatched to Britain to stabilise the situation by A.D. 369. He appears to have undertaken a thorough reconstruction of much of the Wall system minus turrets and outpost forts but with at least some milefortlets in commission. The system seems to have functioned until A.D. 383 when Magnus Maximus perhaps removed much of the army from the north to support his attempted usurpation. Up to that time it is certain from the amount of post-Picts War pottery that forts at Housesteads, Vindolanda and Birdoswald in the central sector of the Wall were occupied in appreciable strength. Although confirmation is yet to come from a modern excavation, this picture can probably be extended westwards into the heart of our area. The hiatus caused by the usurper Magnus Maximus does not appear to have paved the way for further major revolt, largely perhaps thanks to the creation of effective buffer states amongst the Votadini, whose chiefs enjoyed Latinised names in the later fourth century, and the Novantes of Galloway, who, justifiably or otherwise, traced their tribal dynasty henceforth from Maximus. Moreover there is evidence to suggest that it was not the Wall garrison that was stripped to swell the usurpers army but the Second Legion and troops from North Wales and perhaps the Pennines. By this time it was increasingly understood that the retention of the mural barrier was not a pure and simple answer in the north. Defence in depth involved a far larger set of interlocking arrangments. A successful campaign by Maximus in the north may explain why these were resilient enough to surmount the difficulties created by his initially successful campaigns on the Continent, and the subsequent collapse of his cause at Aquileia in 388. It was not apparently until A.D. 396–8 that large scale intervention was again required, this time from the Vandal general Stilicho operating on behalf of the emperor Honorius. To judge from the only source, the poetry of Claudian, the enemies on this occasion were the same Saxons, Picts, and Irish raiders spotting the gap left by Maximus in Gwynedd. To integrate the combined defensive operations Stilicho created the post of *comes Britanniarum*. By A.D. 409 the holder of the post and the other generals and administrators had left, or, more strictly, been expelled from the country by a resurgent British nationalism fuelled by the genuine need to protect the major population centres.[15]

The Christian Dark Age

With the abandonment of the Roman military installations in the late fourth and early fifth centuries the succession of dateable artefacts on archaeological sites in North West England abruptly ceases. There is no identifiable coinage available again in the area before the eighth century at the earliest, and no Carvetian site has yet produced the imported fine wares that have characterised 'Dark Age' settlements of high social status in Wales and south-western England. No strictly historical documentary evidence is available for the fifth century besides the works of Patrick and Gildas, and only a small corpus of verse, and annals surviving in late copies, for the late sixth and early seventh centuries. We are, therefore, for the most part dealing not with historical certainties for this period, but with an array of uncertainty that graduates no further than from the possible to the probable.

Fresh archaeological evidence, though welcome enough, often lacks precise dating, and in any case practically none of the new information relates to the North-West. There is a possible literary hint of occupation, presumably civilian, at Old Carlisle in the fifth century; otherwise only on the Blackfriars site at Carlisle is there evidence of buildings that probably attest the continuation of urban life into the fifth century. Places like Burgh-by-Sands are obvious sites where some continuity of occupation, or re-use, is likely but no Wall site with well-preserved stratigraphy has yet been examined using modern excavation techniques to the best available standards. The archaeological story from the fifth century has yet to emerge, and speculation has tended to surround the few documentary references surviving. Of these, the most significant for our area are the works of St. Patrick, and the hagiography that has been woven around him. It has been argued that St. Patrick was a native of the Irthing valley, perhaps from Birdoswald, the grandson of a priest, the son of a farmer, Calpornius, who was the occupant of a *villula*, and both a deacon and a *decurio* – presumably at Carlisle close by. This interpretation rests on the identification of a *vicus Bana*

(venta) Berniae – the vicus attached to Banna – with Birdoswald or Castlesteads,[16] and suggests a landowning class
possibly with civic responsibilities present in the fifth century,
comparable to that in existence in the Roman period as
demonstrated, for example, by the inscription naming Flavius
Martius as a *decurio* found at Old Penrith. Ravenglass, or
Glannaventa, should not be forgotten as an alternative for
Patrick's home. Its position on the coast would help explain
the capture of Patrick, conceivably during the raids of Niall of
the Nine Hostages in A.D. 405.

Slightly more evidence is available regarding the development of the early Christian church in the area, although again
still without any real chronological precision. St. Ninian is
accredited with launching a mission to this area, and Southern Pictland. Although the rather unlikely site of Whithorn is
usually given as his major seat, it has been suggested that he
centred the diocese at Carlisle, and that the church of St.
Cuthbert at least might date to this period. After all, the city
has claims to have been a provincial capital. There is as yet no
archaeological confirmation of this. For firm evidence, we
must go to the edges of the presumed diocese, to the south and
northwest, where a Christian community can be inferred from
the distribution of sepulchral stones. Along the coast of
Galloway lay a remarkable series of early Christian settlements extending from Kirkmadrine on the Rhinns of Galloway, or nearby at Drummore, to Whithorn and the Isle of
Whithorn, Ardwall Island, Hoddom, and Ruthwell. This
chain of sites has provided one of the most important collec-
tions of early Christian evidence from the Irish Sea province
(Fig. 47). The Kirkmadrine stones, for instance, attest the
presence of *sacerdotes*, or 'priests' with latinised names. Further
to the east on the edge of the Machars lie the two Whithorns,
one on the coast, the other a few kilometres inland. From the
latter comes one of the earliest inscriptions of its kind, in
which Christian significance is evident in the words of its
preamble *'Te deum laudamus'* (= we praise thee, O Lord). Its
regular lettering and ordered presentation commemorates the
death of Latinus (aged 35) and his unnamed daughter and
records his nephew or grandson, Barrovadus, as the man who
set up the memorial.[17]

Fig. 47 Celtic Christian inscribed stones from South West Scotland.
Hayle, in Cornwall, is included here only for comparative purposes (after
Thomas c.1971, The Early Christian Archaeology of North Britain (OUP)).

The inscription was found amongst a cemetery of extended inhumation graves grouped round a small oratory, the walls of which were probably coated in white plaster, thus explaining the name of *Casa Candida*, or White House, traditionally associated with St Ninian's early Christian community in the Whithorn area. A further part of the community was probably formed by the small stone chapel set outside the entrance to the hillfort at Whithorn. The general setting is reminiscent of the early Christian chapel at Balladoole on the Isle of Man. The stone structure still visible today dating from the eighth/ninth century probably overlies the remains of a wooden oratory and the sequence unravelled at Ardwall may well be typical of such sites as Isle of Whithorn where only the later church is known.[18]

Further east two other early Christian sites give a further insight into the kind of archaeological evidence recoverable from this period. The earliest dedication to Saint Kentigern appears to be at Hoddom, a few kilometres north of Annan, although any St. Kentigern dedication in this area may be of the tenth or eleventh centuries rather than earlier. The site can be identified immediately to the east of Hoddom Bridge and aerial photography has recently shown that the detached graveyard currently visible on the ground was in reality associated with a larger elliptical compound possibly containing both religious and secular structures. This pattern has also been recognised at the other nearby Christian site of Ruthwall with its famous cross.[19] The present small church can be seen to lie within an elliptical enclosure similar to that at Hoddom. We can perhaps expand the picture elsewhere. At Old Church Brampton, the dedication to Saint Martin (whose example had inspired Saint Ninian) may indicate the presence of an early religious establishment of some kind within the enclosure of the old Stanegate fort. The fullest information, however, derives from Ninkirk, near Penrith. The present church stands isolated in a sheltered bend of the River Eamont, and has traditional links with Saint Ninian, hence its early name prior to re-dedication to Saint Wilfred sometime before the thirteenth century.[20] Whether the present church stands on the site of the earliest structure is not clear; alongside it, however, crop marks in drought conditions indicate the outline of an elliptical enclosure (Fig. 48). In this case, moreover, it is also possible to discern details of the internal layout. A series of rectangular or sub-rectangular structures occur along the inside edge of the enclosure bank and faint traces indicate the presence of several others. It may be that here we have the site of a pre-English monastic site, although the proposed coin dating has recently been refuted. It is not possible to ascertain whether any of the central structures resemble a church. It is therefore pointless to speculate at the moment whether any original, early church lay within the enclosure or outside it, beneath the surviving church structure. Nor, without excavation, can we speculate usefully about the date, save that the cropmark evidence is comparable to the presumed early example of a monastic site at Hoddom, and perhaps Ruthwell. More significant, perhaps, is the spread of the Christian evidence from the Rhinns of Galloway to the

Fig. 48   The possible Celtic monastery site at Ninkirk, Brougham

upper Eden valley. It seems possible that these sites are coincident with the boundaries of the late sixth century kingdom of Rheged (see further p. 133), and it seems likely that many more cemeteries and church sites of this period will be found in the future, now that objective dating techniques can dispel the chronological problems which still bedevil such candidates as Eaglesfield.[21]

Under the sub-Roman kings, monastic foundations or some local equivalent of the early Welsh *llan* structure, probably played a crucial role in Christian organisation. Monastic settlement had reached southern Ireland and Wales by the early sixth century. It seems likely that the sites in Carvetian territory were comparable in nature, and were coming into being by the mid sixth century. Unfortunately, the recent demolition of the dating of the Ninkirk coin hoard has removed the most objective chronological pointer so far offered, placing it in an uncompromisingly Roman context. While this does suggest some sort of occupation of the church site in the third century there is no evidence to suggest any religious context at this stage. Chronological problems also beset the identification of a ditched enclosure at Ruthwell. Timber from low down from a section across the ditch provided a late prehistoric date.[22]

What should, perhaps, be noted is the apparent vigour of the dark-age Christian community in this area. Despite the incidence of re-dedication, and the lack of the type of documentary evidence that has often provided important information on the Welsh church, the number and density of sites is unprecedented in England. However, problems abound. For example, the distribution of dedications to St. Kentigern (or Mungo) between the Solway and the River Eamont has been offered as evidence for a late stage in the re-establishment of the Celtic church during the expansion of Strathclyde in the tenth century, rather than as a phase of primary dedications.[23] The majority of parish church dedications are to saints with a popularity that runs, if fitfully, from the seventy or eighth centuries as late, in some cases, as the thirteenth.

The Kingdom of Rheged, is known as one of the ultimate, successor kingdoms of Roman imperial authority in the

Pennines and rose to leadership, if not hegemony, under its most powerful king, Urien. The exact location of Rheged has never been established, and was probably in any case somewhat variable under the exigencies of warfare and partible inheritance. It is normally assumed to have been based on the Solway, with the most likely seat of authority at Carlisle, the old *civitas* capital. Such an assumption may well be invalid, at least so far as the royal base is concerned, as in other kingdoms, and notably at Gwynedd, an increasing tendency was underway for decentralisation of the organs of government, with royal or aristocratic 'palaces' scattered on estates throughout the realm. A case has been made on documentary evidence for such a site near the Lyvennet Beck, Crosby Ravensworth, but the site suggested (Cow Green) is an unlikely candidate. Another possibility is the 'Park Pale', a banked enclosure of over twelve acres (5 ha.) with a substantial central building platform, close to the medieval township and church.[24] Even so, the latter may have been, as its name suggests, a medieval buck pasture. The argument is based on the identification of Llwyfenydd with Lyvennet, in a context that might denote either a stream or an estate centre, in association with a royal estate mentioned as providing a source of reward for the poet who was in this case Taliesin. Elsewhere there is a bare scatter of possible sites, Dun Ragit near Stranrear, in the Rhinns of Galloway, Dunmallard at the foot of Ullswater, Rochdale (*Recedham* in Domesday Book), and Treales on the Ribble estuary. Of these, *Recedham* is unlikely, and most of the names of the Dunmallard type are probably the product of the tenth century reintroduction of the Brittonic and Goedelic languages.

Coincident with the problem of site location is the problem of the extent of the successor kingdom. Clearly its northern frontier must have marched with that of the kingdoms centred on Dumbarton in Strathclyde and Ceredig (Selkirkshire), on topographical grounds, perhaps therefore, roughly on the line of the old county boundaries between Wigtown, Kirkcudbright and Dumfries on the south side, and Ayr, Lanark, Peebles and Selkirk to the north. However, the Arthuret battle implies other lost kingdoms north of the Solway. The Pennines provide an obvious boundary to the east, where the

Anglian kingdoms of Bernicia and Deira were established by
the late sixth century, and derived from populations present in
the fifth century. However, Urien was king also in *Catraeth*
(Catterick), modern Richmondshire. Major problems con-
front us to the south-east and south. The extent or existence of
any kingdom based on York in the fifth century is unclear, but
some such power may initially have incorporated the area of
authority of the *Dux Britanniarum* attested in the *Notitia
Dignitatum* (p. 123).

The Harleian genealogies do not provide a historical record
before the generation of Urien of Rheged, and it is *a priori*
unlikely that *Coel Hen* (Old King Cole) is to be associated with
York, or with the numerous dynasties for which he is later
held responsible in the Pennines, by ninth century Welsh
systematisers. Urien himself may derive from non-royal blood
– there is a hint that he was 'elected' by the warband, in which
case his pedigree need not be distinguished. Nor need Rheged
have long enjoyed a recognisable existence before his reign in
the later sixth century . In the south the borders of Rheged are
even more obscure. No British South Pennine kingdom is
known, with the exception of Elmet, in the late sixth and early
seventh centuries. However, by about 600 the fragmentation
of the northern Britons had proceeded sufficiently for the
existence of numerous separate principalities, of which several
are found in the poetic record in Urien's day.[25] It has been
suggested that Rheged in the late sixth century stretched as
far south as Shropshire, thereby incorporating the vacuum
within the distribution of the British kingdoms which is
acknowledged in the Mersey basin east of Powys,[26] but this
seems unlikely. The possibility that Rheged was under some
pressure from pagan Anglo-Saxon communities in Yorkshire
in the 6th century is born out by the scatter of diagnostic
burials under mounds along the Lune-Eden watershed.

Dark Age settlement and economy

Despite the virulence of sixth century warfare and raiding, we
can only guess at the population and economy of the Solway
area during this two-century epoch. At no single site has
occupation yet been established for any significant stretch of

this period, although, as stated, in Carlisle itself, documentary evidence at least supports reoccupation in the seventh century (p. 52), and the hypothesis of a fifth century population is now receiving some archaeological support. Elsewhere, archaeologists have yet to respond to the challenge of locating and excavating the crucial sites. The size of the rural population is also a matter of guesswork. Obviously, a king capable of raiding and campaigning in the Lothians, at Bamburgh and Lindisfarne, and, conceivably, in Powys must have drawn upon a substantial force of warriors, who themselves were necessarily supported by a far larger body of peasants. A discussion of population density in a period where the rural communities appear to have been aceramic in culture has few points of departure. Perhaps the most obvious is the size of the armies which were taking part in the campaigns of Urien and Owain his son. The implications underlying most studies is that the normal army was a very small body of men, numbered in hundreds and not thousands, travelling and fighting on horseback and both well-armed and well-trained. Such a view is at least superficially supported by the most considerable relevant text – the Gododdin – that recounts the campaign fought at *Catreath* (= Catterick) by an army of about 300 men from Edinburgh. Jackson, however, in the most comprehensive study yet undertaken of this poem, argued for a total armed force of up to ten times this number.[27] If we should take account of his arguments, and assume a basic parity between the resources of Mynyddog of Edinburgh and Urien, late sixth century Rheged must have had a total population hardly less than 30,000 adult males, or 100,000 *in toto* of which the original Carvetian territory might have had a third or a half. There is therefore little reason on the face of it to assume a substantial loss of population in the post-Roman era, at least prior to the Northumbrian absorption of the Western Pennines. The evidence from pollen diagrams also suggests that agriculture and pastoral land-use continued from the late Roman period without discernable break until about A.D. 600 or even later.[28]

The common tendency is to credit the great plague of the mid-fifth century with a permanent impact on the British population and to suggest that it was in some way responsible for the British collapse and Anglo-Saxon conquest. While a plague of this nature may have had a serious demographic and social impact, there seems no reason to exempt the Anglian kingdoms from similar problems, nor to look to this phenomenon as a major factor in long-term political eventualities.[29]

It is equally unclear what style of settlement the sub-Roman population occupied, and how they supported themselves. It has already been noticed that a changeover occurred during the latter half of the Roman occupation from a roundhouse habitation tradition to a rectilinear timber post or stone walled building style. At the Penrith Romano-British site at Crossfield (p. 95) such a 'house' was occupied into the middle of the fourth century, at which stage the pottery evidence ceases. Elsewhere it has proved impossible as yet to date the period of occupation of such 'houses', particularly in the upland zone where a stone building tradition is dominant. A rash of such sites has recently been located along the watershed between the Eden and Lune valleys,[30] in addition to those already known at Crosby Ravensworth, where they were assumed to be a product of Anglian colonisation. Such an 'ethnic' interpretation of settlement history is unnecessary and ill-supported by the evidence. Comparable rectilinear structures comprising the ultimate phase in rural settlement occupation in marginal terrains are known throughout the Pennines. Although the only one yet to be fully excavated – at Ribblehead – has produced a ninth century occupation date,[31] it seems likely that we are dealing with a long-lived tradition of building, and one that at this stage had no logical break with late Roman traditions.

While there does seem to have been a certain amount of abandonment of arable land in marginal terrains already underway in the late Roman period, two factors suggest a continuing agricultural production into the sixth century. The rather nominal presence of cereal pollens in the few lake sediment cores that have been examined continues to about A.D. 800 and this somewhat ephemereal evidence receives support from one poetic source in which Urien is described as 'Lord of the cultivated plain'.[32] Such a description is unlikely if no widescale agriculture was taking place, but might refer either to cultivation in the Solway Plain and Eden valley or conceivably to the Fylde and lower Lune valley. In either case, what evidence is available seems to suggest a continuing agricultural output at least in the better favoured areas, that must infer a relatively settled lifestyle, with the occupation of permanent sites and established resource territories. The grant of Carlisle, with a 15 mile radius surrounding area and with its Britons, to St Cuthbert in A.D. 685 seems to confirm this picture of a settled agricultural landscape.[33]

It has also been argued that the early medieval estate structure found throughout the Pennines is derived from Celtic origins, and shares crucial similarities with that of Wales.[34] The scanty early estate evidence from West of the Pennines tends to support this argument both on the Solway and in Lancashire, and it seems likely that a substantial, if unfree, Celtic population in former Rheged carried over into the seventh century, and survived the advent of English political, religious and social control.[35]

Clearly, some monastic foundations such as Ecclefechan and Heversham were of Anglian or later date. For example, Bede mentions the foundation of a monastery at Dacre (near Penrith) in a context which suggests that it occurred within his adult lifetime.[36] No certain trace of the site has yet been found in the recent excavations at Dacre Church, but aceramic occupation of at least one, rectangular, timber framed building is likely to be pre Conquest at least. On the whole, the Anglicanisation of the church of Rheged during the seventh century has left little mark outside the inscribed stones, and it should be borne in mind that the Northumbrian church was Celtic in inspiration, if eventually Anglian in personnel. The Carlisle diocese may have either survived the advent of Northumbrian control or been recreated, passing from ecclesiastical prehistory under the royal house of Rheged to become an appointment that was exclusively English, but one which was in existence as late as the early tenth century.

On the whole then, the weight of the admittedly, largely inferential, evidence supports the survival of a peasantry and aristocracy into the sub-Roman period, capable of forming the basis of a strong successor state as late as the last quarter of the sixth century. There is no evidence that the peasant population of this epoch was seriously affected by the Northumbrian absorption or conquest, whichever occurred, during the early seventh century. Positive evidence for genocide is insubstantial, and place-name evidence is far less consistent with an Anglian peasant colonisation that has been thought. On the whole, large scale survival of this ethnic group into the Nortumbrian era seems highly likely – and desirable from the point of view of an incoming aristocracy in need of a servile labour force. Recent work on modern blood group distributions demonstrates a similarity between the Cumbrian population and that of central Wales that can only have resulted from a common ethnic stock,[37] and it is to the lowest, and largest, status groups in British society that we should look for the continuity of settlement in the sub-Roman period that these factors suggest.

Notes and References

References to British journals use the abbreviations recommended by the Council for British Archaeology, which are those of the American Standards Association (list 239, 5–1963 revised 1966). Other abbreviations used are:

CIL   *Corpus Inscriptionum Latinarum*
CW₁   Cumberland & Westmorland Archaeological and Anti-
                quarian Society, Old Series.
CW₂   Cumberland & Westmorland Archaeological and Anti-
                quarian Society, New Series.
D & G Trans.   Transactions of the Dumfries & Galloway Natural History
                and Antiquarian Society.
Handbook   J. Collingwood Bruce *Handbook to the Roman Wall*: (13th.
                Edited and enlarged by C.M. Daniels, 1978).
RIB   R.G. Collingwood and P.W. Wright *Roman Inscriptions of
                Britain* i (Oxford 1965).

1.   TRIBAL TERRITORY AND THE PRE-ROMAN IRON AGE

1.   Ministry of Agriculture, Agricultural Land Services Technology Report xi *1974*, 7.
2.   Pennington *1970*, 77.
3.   McK Clough *1969*, 1.
4.   Burl *1970*, 16.
5.   Collingwood *1938*, 32.
6.   Higham *1981*, 1.
7.   Blake *1960*, Collingwood *1933*, 219.
8.   Higham *1978*b, 143.
9.   Smith *1978*, 19ff.
10. Juvenal *Satires* XIV, 196; Seneca *Apocolocyntosis* 12. See also Ptolemy *Geog.* 2.3.10 and Tacitus *Agricola* 17. Pausanias' use of the tribal name (*Descr. Graecae* VIII, 43) presents a much disputed textual crux. For the Brigantes in general see B.R. Hartley's forthcoming companion study in this series and for the tribal boundaries, E. Birley *1961*, 30.
11. For the Parisi in general use see H. Ramm *The Parisi* (1978).

12. Birley, A.R. *Northern History* 1980.
13. *RIB* 933.
14. *J. Roman Stud.* lv (1965), 224.
15. *RIB* 311; compare *RIB* 288 from the cantonal capital of the Cornovii at Wroxeter.
16. Agricultural Land Classification of England & Wales – Grade 2.
17. *RIB* 772, 773, 774, 775, 776, 777, and *J. Roman Stud.* lix (1969) 237.
18. A transect of a cemetery north-west of the fort has been excavated in advance of roadworks.
19. Ross *1967*, 4666; cf. Ross *1961*, 63. The likeliest origin of the tribal name appears to lie in the root *Cer* which appears in the name of the horned god *Cernunnos*.
20. Tacitus *Annals* XII, 32, 36, 40; *Histories* III, 45.
21. Wheeler *1954*.
22. Tacitus *Agricola*, 17.
23. Stukeley *It. Curiosum*, 1724.
24. *RIB* 2283; for a recorded distance from a major centre see *RIB* 2243, 2244.
25. Birley, E. *1953*a.
26. Birley, E. *1961*, 36; Frere *1974*, 71; *Ross* 1967, 452.
27. The Solway is fordable at the Sandwath north of Burgh-by-Sands.
28. *RIB* 908.
29. *RIB* 923.

2. HISTORY: A.D. 43–367

1. *CW*$_2$ 34 (1934), 50.
2. Richmond and Crawford *1949*, 48.
3. See further p.   .
4. *Britannia* x (1979) 283.
5. Bellhouse *1956*, 28; excavation of the defences by Miss Charlesworth.
6. 'The South Gate of the Roman Fort at Carlisle', *Roman Frontier Studies Congress 1979* BAR 71 (1980), 201ff.
7. Information kindly provided by Drs. A.K. Bowman and J.D. Thomas. See now Bowman and Thomas, 1983.
8. *CW*$_2$ 77 (1977), 39ff.; cf. *CW*$_2$ 58 (1958), 31; *CW*$_2$ 62 (1962), 73.
9. Potter *1979*, 176ff.
10. Potter *1979*, 357.
11. *CW*$_2$ 51 (1951), 34ff.; 65 (1965), 102ff.
12. Breeze and Dobson, *1978*.
13. *Britannia* ix (1978) 418.
14. *CIL* XI, 5213 records a *censitor Britonnum Anavonensium*; for *Anava* = R. Annan see Rivet and Smith *1979*, 249.
15. Bowman, A.K. and Thomas, J.D.*1983*, 110.
16. *Archaeologia Aeliana*,[4] xli (1963) 51; cf. xlix (1971) 19.
17. *Britannia* ix (1978), 423; x (1979), 282 fig. 5.
18. Jones, G.D.B. *1979*, 85; 1982, 282ff.

19. CW_2 73 (1973), 126ff.; 75 (1975), 58ff. See also Jones G.D.B. 1982, 282ff.
20. See p. 35.
21. Bellhouse 1962, 56ff.
22. Jones, G.D.B. 1975, 20; 1976, 236ff.
23. Britannia x (1979), 424; Jones G.D.B. 1982, 282ff.
24. Handbook, 198.
25. CW_2 35 (1935), 220; J. Roman Stud. xxv (1935) 1.
26. CW_2 53 (1953), 22.
27. Pottery from Burgh-by-Sands I, kindly examined by John Gillam; for Bewcastle see Potter 1979, 327.
28. CW_2 54 (1954), 36ff.; 63 (1963), 140ff.; 70 (1970), 42ff.
29. CW_2 47 (1947), 85ff.; Potter 1947, 149ff.
30. CW_2 69 (1969), 57; 57 (1957), 8; 70 (1970), 21.
31. CW_2 65 (1965), 102ff.; 64 (1964), 63ff.; 77 (1977), 17ff.
32. Actual evidence of Severan campaigning along the west coast route is now known in the form of the 63-acre marching camp at Kirkpatrick Fleming near Gretna. A.R. Birley (Septimius Severus (1971) 265ff.) has shown the connection between the unit of Moorish soldiers at Burgh-by-Sands and the account contained in Historia Augusta: Severus xxii, 1–7.
33. Jarrett 1976, 39ff.; Potter 1979, 363.

3. COMMUNICATIONS AND URBAN SETTLEMENT

1. In general, see I.D. Margary, Roman Roads in Britain (1967).
2. Bulmer, 1885, 16ff.
3. Bellhouse 1956a, 37.
4. Richmond 1951, 293ff.
5. CW_2 31 (1931), 111.
6. Excavation by the authors in 1976.
7. Observation by the first author.
8. Richmond 1951, 300ff.
9. Information from Professor J.K. St. Joseph.
10. For Carlisle in general see Clack and Gosling 1976, 165; Charlesworth 1978, 115 with full bibliography. For the Vindolanda writing tablet, see Bowman, AK. and Thomas, J.D. 1983, 110. For recent work in Carlisle see Britannia 82, 79–91.
11. Salway 1965, 41ff.
12. RIB 899.
13. Higham and Jones 1975, 21ff.; See earlier Salway 1965, 114ff. and Birley, E. 1951, 16ff. Jones G.D.B., 1983, 1984.
14. For details of the situation at Vindolanda see Birley, R.E. 1978
15. Jones, G.D.B.1979a, 28ff.
16. CW_2 29 (1929), 311; 32 (1932), 141; 33 (1933), 246; 34 (1934), 120; Salway 1965, 96.
17. Ravenna Cosmography 155.

18. Birley, E. *1946*, 27ff; Salway *1965*, 129ff.
19. P. Austin, personal communication.
20. Salway *1965*, 135ff.
21. Richmond and Crawford *1949*, 15; Radford *1952*, 35; Rivet and Smith *1979*, 395.

4. RURAL SETTLEMENT

1. Higham and Jones *1975*, 21ff and fig. 4.
2. Jones, G.D.B. *1979*, 83ff; Jones, G.D.B. *1980*, 62ff.
3. Richmond and Crawford *1949*, 22.
4. Radford *1952*, 35.
5. *J. Roman Stud.* li (1961), 61.
6. e.g. Smith *1977*, 126ff.
7. Webster, R.A. *1971*, 64.
8. Blake *1960*, 5ff.
9. *Historia Augusta: Hadrian* xi.
10. Hay *1945*, 126.
11. R.C.H.M. *1936*, 254; Higham *1980*, 44, *1983*, 49.
12. R.C.H.M. *1936*, 105; Higham *1978*b, 147ff.
13. R.C.H.M. *1936*, 75; Jones, G.D.B. *1975*a 95; Higham *1978*a, 119.
14. Higham *1978*a, 123.
15. R.C.H.M. *1936*, 103; Webster, R.A. *1972*, 66; Jones, G.D.B. *1975*a, 95; Higham *1978*b, 146.
16. Higham *1978*b, 142.
17. Higham and Jones *1975*, 39.
18. Collingwood, R.G. *1933*, 201; R.C.H.M. *1936*, 83.
19. Higham *1978*a, 125.
20. Collingwood, W.G. *1909*, 295ff.
21. Lowndes *1963*, fig. 2.
22. Lowndes *1964*, 6ff; Higham *1979*a, 34.
23. Higham *1978*b, 151.
24. Higham *1978*a, fig. 16.6.
25. Higham *1982*a, 29.
26. Collingwood, W.G. *1909*, 295.
27. Lowndes *1964*, 6.
28. Webster, R.A. *1972*, 66.
29. Blake, *1960*, 1ff.
30. Higham and Jones, 1983, 62.
31. Higham, *1981*, fig. 4.

5. INDUSTRY AND THE ECONOMY

1. Higham *1980*, 44; *1983*, 49
2. Higham *1978*a, 121.
3. Collingwood *1909*, 306; Blake *1960*, 10.

4. Bowman and Thomas *1974*, 28.
5. Renfrew *1973*, Pl. 3, Higham *1982*a, 32.
6. Piggott *1958*, 13ff.
7. Higham *1978*b, 147.
8. Lindquist *1974*, 29.
9. e.g. Hodgson *1968* 127; McDonald and Curle *1928–9*, 568ff.
10. Lindquist *1974*, 27ff.
11. Polybius *VI* 39.13.
12. Bowman and Thomas *1974*, 28.
13. Clark and Haswell *1964*, 192.
14. Davies *1976*, 271.
15. Higham *1982* fig 17; Higham and Jones *1983*; Blake *1960*, 3ff.
16. Manning *1975*, 114.
17. Gillam *1973*, 53ff.
18. See p. 52.
19. Gillam *1973*, 54ff; Webster, P. *1979*, 15ff.
20. Webster, P. *1972*, 191.
21. Blake, *1960*.
22. *RIB* 1952.
23. *RIB* 1008.
24. *RIB* 998–1000.
25. Phillips *1976* 101ff.
26. *RIB* 758.
27. Antiq. J. xlix (1969) 224ff; *J. Roman Stud.* lx (1970) 169ff.
28. *CW₂* 31 (1931), 81ff.
29. *J. Roman Stud.* lx (1970), 180ff.

6. THE LATE FOURTH AND FIFTH CENTURIES

1. Herodian *III*, 8.1.
2. Birley, E. *1953*, 52.
3. Birley, A.R., *forthcoming*.
4. Ammianus *28*, 3, 7.
5. Jones *1975*a, 100.
6. *RIB* 1576, 1594.
7. *Archaeologia Aeliana*,⁵ vii (1979) 127.
8. cf. Frere *1974*, 263, fig. 11.
9. Jones and Shotter, *forthcoming*.
10. Ammianus *28*, 3, 8. (Sometimes known as areani.)
11. For a fuller discussion see Frere *1974*, 391.
12. See note 10.
13. For the most recent discussion see Jones, G.D.B. *1980*, 62ff.
14. Jones, G.D.B. *1980*, 66.
15. Frere *1974*, 408.
16. Thomas, A.C. 'St Patrick and Fifth Century Britain' *in* Casey, P.J. (Ed.) *The End of Roman britain* (BAR 71) 1979, 81ff; for *Banna* see M.J. Hassall 'Britain in the Notitia Dignitatum', Goodburn and Barth-

olomew (Eds.), *Aspects of the Notitia Dignitatum* (BAR S15), 1976, 103ff.
17. Thomas *1971*, 12ff.
18. Thomas *1971*, 72ff.
19. Jones, G.D.B. *in* Proudfoot, E. (Ed.) *Discovery and Excavation in Scotland 1979* (Edinburgh).
20. Bouch *1956*, 108.
21. Wilson *1978*, 47.
22. Casey, P. *Britannia* ix (1978) 23. At Ruthwell the ditch was sectioned by C. Crowe to whom we are indebted for permission to include this information. Timber from the ditch in Church Glebe Field gave a date of 370±80 b.c. (HAR 4457).
23. Bowen, E.G. *1969*, 87.
24. Hogg, A.H.A. *1946*, 211; see now Higham *1979*b, 45.
25. Jackson *1969*, Introduction. See also *Bull. Board. Celt. Stud.* xxvi (1975) III, 255–80.
26. Morris *1973*, 209.
27. Jackson *1969*, 13.
28. Pennington *1970*, 77.
29. Morris *1973*, 169ff; *Britannia* viii (1977) 319.
30. Higham *1979*a, 34.
31. King *1978*, 21.
32. Shaw *1964*, 28.
33. V.C.H. II, 4.
34. Jones, G.J.R. *1965*, 67ff.
35. Higham *1979*b, 50.
36. Bede *IV*, 32.
37. Potts *1976*, 242.

Bibliography

Bellhouse, R.L. (1955), The Roman Fort at Burrow Walls, CW_2 lv, 30.
Bellhouse, R.L. (1956), The Roman Temporary Camps near Troutbeck, Cumberland, CW_2 lvi, 28.
Bellhouse, R.L. (1956a), Some Roman Roads in Cumberland, CW_2 lvii, 37.
Bellhouse, R.L. (1958), Some Fieldwork at Caermote, CW_2 lvii, 27–29.
Bellhouse, R.L. (1960), Roman Forts near Caermote, CW_2 lx, 20.
Bellhouse, R.L. (1960a), Excavations at Old Carlisle, CW_2 lix, 15–31.
Bellhouse, R.L. (1961), An Earthwork in Kirkbampton Parish, CW_2 lxi, 42.
Bellhouse, R.L. (1962), Morecambe in Roman Times and Roman Sites on the Cumberland Coast, CW_2 lxii, 56–72.
Bellhouse, R.L. (1967), The Aughertree Fell Enclosures, CW_2 lxvii, 26–30.
Bellhouse, R.L. (1971), Roman Tileries at Scalesceugh and Brampton CW_2 lxxi, 79.
Bellhouse, R.L. and Richardson, G.G.S. (1975), The Roman Site at Kirkbride, Cumberland, CW_2 lxxv, 58.
Birley, A.R. (1967), Review of the *Frontier People of Roman Britain, Northern History*, ii, 148–150.
Birley, A.R. (1967a), The Roman Governors of Britain, *Epigrapische Studien* iv, 6.
Birley, A.R. (1973), Petillius Cerialis and the Conquest of Brigantia, *Britannia* iv, 179–190.
Birley, A.R. (1979), *The People of Roman Britain* (London).
Birley, E. (1946), Old Penrith and its Problems, CW_2 xlvi, 27–38.
Birley, E. (1951), The Roman Fort and Settlement at Old Carlisle, CW_2 li, 16–39.
Birley, E (1953), Civil Settlements on Hadrian's Wall, in E. Birley, *Roman Britain and the Roman Army*, (Kendal), 69.
Birley, E. (1953a), The Roman Milestone at Middleton-in-Lonsdale, CW_2 liii, 52.
Birley, E. (1961), *Roman Britain and the Roman Army*.
Birley, R.E. (1978), *Vindolanda* (London).
Blake, B. (1960), Excavations of Native (Iron Age) sites in Cumberland, CW_2 lix, 1–14.
Bouch, C.M.L. (1950), Ninkirk, Brougham, CW_2 l, 80–90.

Bouch, C.M.L. (1956), A Dark Age Coin Hoard from Ninkirk, *CW₂* lv, 108–111.

Bowen, E.G. (1969), *Saints, Seaways and Settlements in the Celtic Lands* (Cardiff).

Bowen, H.C. (1962), *Ancient Fields* (London).

Bowman, A.K. and Thomas, J.D. (1974), *The Vindolanda Writing Tablets* (Newcastle-upon-Tyne).

Bowman, A.K. and Thomas, J.D. (1983) *The Vindolanda Writing Tablets* (London).

Breeze, D.J. and Dobson, B. (1978), *Hadrian's Wall* (London).

Bulmer, T. (1885), *History, Topography and Directory of Westmorland* (London).

Burl, H.A.W. (1970), Henges, internal features and regional groups, *Archaeological Journal*, cxxvi, 1.

Bushe-Fox, J.P. (1913), The use of Samian pottery in the dating of the early occupation at Carlisle, *Archaeologia*, lxiv, 295.

Casey, P.J. (1978), The Ninekirks (Brougham) hoard; a re-consideration, *CW₂*, lxxviii, 23–28.

Charlesworth, D. (1978), Roman Carlisle, *Archaeological Journal*, cxxxv, 115.

Clack, C. and Haswell, M. (1964), *The Economics of Subsistence Agriculture* (London).

Clack, P.A.G. and Gosling, P.F. (1976), *Archaeology in the North* (Durham).

Clare, T. (1981), The Evidence for continuity in Cumbria in P. Clack and S. Haselgrove (Eds) *Rural Settlement in the Roman North* (Durham) 43–56.

Collingwood, R.G. (1933a), An introduction to the Prehistory of Cumberland, Westmorland and Lancashire North of the Sands, *CW₂* xxxiii, 163.

Collingwood, R.G. (1933b), Prehistoric settlements near Crosby Ravensworth, *CW₂* xxxiii, 201.

Collingwood, R.G. (1938), The Hillfort on Carrock Fell, *CW₂* xxxviii, 32.

Collingwood, R.G. and Wright, R.P. (1965), *Roman Inscriptions of Britain* I (Oxford).

Collingwood, W.G. (1909), Report on a further exploration of the Romano-British settlement at Ewe Close, Crosby Ravensworth, *CW₂* ix, 295.

Cramp, R. (1983), Anglo-Saxon Settlement *BAR* 118, 263–298.

Davies, R. (1977), Ateco of Old Carlisle, *Britannia* viii, 271.

Dymand, C.W. (1893), An Ancient Village in Hugill, *CW₁* xii, 6–14.

Elliot, G. (1973), Field Systems of Northwest England, in A.R.H. Baker and R.A. Butlin (Eds.) *Studies in Field Systems in the British Isles* (Cambridge) 41–92.

Feachem, R.W. (1973), Ancient Agriculture in the Highland Zone of Britain, *Proc. of the Prehist. Soc.* xxxix, 332–354.

Fell, C.I. (1972), *Early Settlement in the Lake Counties* (Clapham).

Fell, C.I. (1974), Short Notes on Unrecorded Finds, *CW2* lxxiv, 1–6.

Ferguson, R. (1874), A Survey of Roman Cumberland and Westmorland, *CW₁* iii, 15–18.

Ferguson, R. (1879), An Attempt at a Survey of Roman Cumberland and Westmorland, *CW₁* iv, 226.

Ferguson, R. (1883), The Bishop's Dyke, Dalston, *CW₁* vii, 271–278.

Ferguson, R. and Cowper, H.S. (1843), Topographical Index of Cumberland and Westmorland, *Archaeologia* liii, 485–538.

Fowler, P.J. (1976), Small Settlements and their Context in Western Britain, first to fifth centuries A.D., *Proc. Royal Irish Acad.* lxxvic, 191–206.

Frere, S.S. (1974), *Britannia* (London).

Garlick, T. (1970), *Romans in the Lake Counties* (Clapham).

Gelling, M. (1974), The Chronology of English Place Names, in T. Rowley, (Ed.) *Anglo-Saxon Settlement and Landscape*, (Oxford) 93–101.

Gillam, J.P. (1973), Sources of Pottery found on Northern Military Sites, in A. Detsicus (Ed.) *Current Research in Romano-British Coarse Pottery*, 53.

Gresham, C.A and Hemp., W.J. (1963) The Interpretation of Settlement Patterns in North West Wales, in L.I. Foster and L. Alcock (eds) *Culture and Environment* (Bristol) 263–280.

Hay, T. (1940), Our Early Settlements and their Physiographic Setting, *CW₂* xl, 136–140.

Hay, T. (1945), Stone Carr, *CW₂* xliv, 126–133.

Higham, N.J. (1976), An Early Medieval Site at Caldbeck, Ravenstonedale, *CW₂* lxxvi, 214–15.

Higham, N.J. (1978a), Early Field Survival in North Cumbria, in H.E. Bowen and P.J. Fowler (Eds.) *Early Land Allotment*, (B.A.R. 48) 119–125.

Higham, N.J. (1978b) Dyke Systems in North Cumbria, *Bull. Board Celtic Studs.* xxviii, 142–155.

Higham, N.J. (1978c) Continuity Studies in the first millenium A.D. in North Cumbria, *Northern History*, xiv, 1–18.

Higham, N.J. (1979a), An Aerial Survey of the Upper Lune Valley in N.J. Higham (Ed.) *The Changing Past* (Manchester) 31.

Higham, N.J. (1979b), Continuity in Northwest England in the First Millenium, in N.J. Higham (Ed.) *The Changing Past* (Manchester) 43.

Higham, N.J. (1980), Rural Settlement West of the Pennines, in K. Branigan (Ed.) *Rome and the Brigantes* (Sheffield) 41–7.

Higham, N.J. (1981), 2 Enclosures at Dobcross Hall, Dalston *CW₂* LXXXI, 1–6.

Higham, N.J. (1982a), Native Settlements on the North Slopes of the Lake District, *CW₂* LXXXII, 29–33.

Higham, N.J. (1982b), The Roman Impact upon rural settlement in Cumbria in P. Clack and S. Hazelgrove (Eds.) *Rural Settlement in the Roman North* (CBA.3).

Higham, N.J. (1983), A Romano-British field system at Yanwath Woodhouse, *CW₂* LXXXIII, 49–58.

Higham, N.J. and Jones, G.D.B. (1975), Frontiers, Forts and Farmers, Cumbrian Aerial Survey 1974–75, *Archaeol. J.* CXXXII, 16–53.

Higham, N.J. and Jones, G.D.B. (1983) Two Romano-British Farm sites in North Cumbria, *Britannia* xiv, 45–72.

Hodgson, G. (1968), A Comparative Account of Animal Remains from Corstopitum and the Iron Age Farm at Catcote, *Archaeologia Aeliana* 4, xlvi, 127–162.

Hodgson, K.S. (1954), Four Querns from the Brampton Area, *CW₂* liii, 209–211.

Hogg, A.H.A. (1946), Llwynfenydd, *Antiquity* xx, 211–212.

Hogg, R. (1949), A Roman Cemetery Site at Beckfoot, Cumberland, CW_2 xlix, 32–37.

Hogg, R. (1952), Historic Crossings of the River Eden at Stanwix and their associated road systems, CW_2 lii, 131.

Hogg, R. (1955), Excavations at Carlisle, 1953, CW_2 lv, 59.

Hogg, R. (1965), Excavations of the Roman auxiliary Tilery, Brampton, CW_2 lxv, 133.

Hogg, R. (1972), Factors affecting the spread of early settlement in the Lake Counties, CW_2 lxxii, 1–35.

Jackson, K.H. (1955), The Britons in South Scotland, *Antiquity* xxix, 77–88.

Jackson, K.H. (1956), *Language and History in Early Britain* (Edinburgh).

Jackson, K.H. (1958), The Sources for the Life of St Kentigern, in N. Chadwick (Ed.) *Studies in the Early British Church* (Cambridge) 273.

Jackson, K.H. (Ed.) (1969), *The Gododdin: The oldest Scottish poem* (Edinburgh).

Jarrett, M.G. (1976), *Maryport, Cumbria: A Roman Fort and its Garrison* (Kendal).

Jensen, G.F. (1973), Place Name Research and Northern History, *Northern History* viii, 1–23.

Jobey, G. (1959), Excavations on a native settlement at Huckhoe, Northumberland, *Archaeologia Aeliana* 4, xxxviii, 217–278.

Jobey, G. (1963), Additional Rectilinear Settlements in Northumberland, *Archaeologia Aeliana* 4, xli, 211–215.

Jobey, G. (1964), Stone-built Settlements in North Northumberland, *Archaeologia Aeliana* 4, xlii, 41–64.

Jobey, G. (1965), Hillforts and Settlements in Northumberland, *Archaeologia Aeliana* 4, xliii, 21–64.

Jobey,, G. (1966), A field Survey in Northumberland, in A.L.F. Rivet (Ed.) *The Iron Age in Northern Britain* (London).

Jobey, G. (1966a), Homesteads and Settlements of the Frontier Area, in C. Thomas (Ed.) *Rural Settlement in Roman Britain* (London), 3ff.

Jobey, G. (1981), Between Tyne and Forth: Some Problems, in P. Clack and S. Haselgrove (Eds) *Rural Settlement in the Roman North* (Durham) 7–20.

Jones, G.D.B. (1968), The Romans in the Northwest, *Northern History*, iii, 1ff..

Jones, G.D.B. (1975a), The North-Western Interface, in P.J. Fowler (Ed.) *Recent Work in Rural Archaeology* (Bradford-upon-Avon) 93–106.

Jones, G.D.B. (1975b), in Higham and Jones, 1975.

Jones, G.D.B. (1976), The Western Extension of Hadrian's Wall: Bowness to Cardurnock, *Britannia*, vii, 236–243.

Jones, G.D.B. (1979a), *Hadrian's Wall from the Air* (Manchester).

Jones, G.D.B. (1979b), The Concept & Development of Roman Frontiers, *Bull. J. Rylands Lib.*, lxi 1, 115ff.

Jones, G.D.B. (1979c), Aerial Photography in the North, in N.J. Higham (Ed.) *The Changing Past* (Manchester) 75.

Jones, G.D.B. (1979), Invasion and Response in Roman Britain, in B. Burnham and H. Johnson (Eds.) *Invasion and Response* (Oxford) 17–31.

Jones, G.D.B. (1980), Archaeology and Coastal Change in the Northwest, in F. Thompson and R. Collins (Eds.) *Coastal Archaeology* (London).

Jones, G.D.B. (1982), The Solway Frontier, *Britannia* xiii, 282–97.

Jones, G.D.B. (1983), Either Side of Solway: towards a Minimalist View of Romano-British Agricultural Settlement in the North-West in J. Chapman and H. Mytum (Eds.), *Settlement in North Britain 1000 B.C.–A.D. 1000* (Oxford) 185–204 (with J. Walker).

Jones, G.D.B. (1984), 'Becoming Different without knowing it', in A. King and T. Blagg (eds.), *Military and Civilian in Roman Britain* (Oxford), forthcoming.

Jones, G.D.B. and Webster, P.V. (1968), *Mediolanum*: Excavations at Whitchurch, *Archaeol. J.* cxxv, 193–254.

Jones, G.J.R. (1960–1), The Pattern of Settlement on the Welsh Borders, *Agric. Hist. Rev.*, viii–ix, 8–9.

Jones, G.J.R. (1961), Basic Patterns of Settlement Distribution in Northern England, *Advancement of Science* xviii, 192–200.

Jones, G.J.R. (1972), *Post Roman Wales* (Cambridge).

Jones, G.J.R. (1975), Early Territorial Organisation in Gwynedd and Elmet, *Northern History* x, 30–41.

Jones, G.J.R. (1976), Multiple Estates and Early Settlement, in P.H. Sawyer (Ed.) *Medieval Settlement* (Cambridge) 15–40.

King, A. (1970), *Early Pennine Settlement* (Clapham).

King, A. (1978), Gauber High Pasture, Ribbleshead — an interim report, in R. Hall (Ed.) *Viking Age York and the North* (London) 21–25.

Kirkby, D.P. (1962), Strathclyde and Cumbria: a survey of historical development to 1092, *CW₂* lxii, 77–94.

Laing, L. (1977), *Celtic Survival* (B.A.R. 37).

Lindquist, Sven-Olaf (1974), The Development of the Agrarian Landscape on Gotland during the Early Iron Age, *Norwegian Archaeol. Rev.* lxxi, 6–31.

Lowdnes, R.A.C. (1963) 'Celtic' fields, farms and burial mounds in the Lune Valley, *CW₂* lxiii, 77–95.

Lowdnes, R.A.C. (1964), Excavations of a Romano-British farmstead at Eller Beck, *CW₂* lxiv, 6–13.

Manning, W.H. (1966), A Hoard of Romano-British Ironwork from Brampton, Cumberland, *CW₂* lxvi, 1–36.

Manning, W.H. (1975), Economic Influences on Land Use in the military areas of the Highland Zonne, in J. Evans et al (Eds.) *The Effects of Man on the Landscape: The Highland Zone* (London) 112–116.

McDonald, G. and Curle, A.O. (1928–9), The Roman Fort at Mumrills near Falkirk, *Proceedings of the Society of Antiquaries, Scotland* vi, lxiii, 396–575.

McCarthy, M.R. (1982) Thomas, Chadwick and Post-Roman Carlisle *BAR* B103, 241–256.

McK Clough, T.H. (1969), Bronze-Age Metalwork from Cumbria, *CW₂* lxix, 1–39.

Ministry of Agriculture, Fisheries and Food (1974), Agricultural Land Classification Technical Reports, *Agricultural Land Classification* (London).

Ministry of Agriculture, Fisheries and Food (1958), *Rations for Livestock*, Bulletin No. 48 (London).

Ministry of Agriculture, Fisheries and Food (1965), *Grass and Grassland*, Bulletin No. 154 (London).

Morris, J. (1973), *The Age of Arthur: a history of the British Isles from 350 to 650* (London).

Myhre, B. (1973), The Iron Age Farm in Southwest Norway, *Norwegian Archaeol. Rev.* vi, n.1, 14–31.

Nicolson, J. and Burn, R. (1777), *A History of the Counties of Cumberland, Westmorland and Lancashire North of the Sands* 2 vols. (London).

Parker, F.H.M. (1905), Inglewood Forest, CW_2 v, 35–61.

Pennington, W. (1970), Vegetational History in the Northwest of England — a regional study, in D. Walker and R. West, (Eds.) *Studies in Vegetational History of the British Isles*, (Cambridge) 41–80.

Philips, C.W. (1970), *The Fenland in Roman Times* (London).

Philips, E.J. (1976) A Workshop of Roman Sculptors at Carlisle, *Britannia* vii, 10.

Piggott, S. (1958), Native Economies and the Roman Occupation of North Britain, in I. Richmond (Ed.) *Roman and Native in North Britain* (Edinburgh and London) 1–27.

Potter, T.W. (1977), The Biglands Milefortlet, *Britannia*, viii, 149.

Potter, T.W. (1979), *Romans in North West England* (Kendal).

Potts, W.T.A. (1976), History and Blood groups in the British Isles in P.H. Sawyer (Ed.) *Medieval Settlement* (London) 236.

Provan, D.M.J. (1973), The Soils of an Iron Age Farm Site, *Norwegian Archaeological Review*, vi, n1, 32–41.

Radford, C.A.R. (1952), Locus Maponi *D and G Trans*, xxxi, 35–38.

Ragg, F.W. (1905), Gospatrick's Charter, CW_2 v, 71–84.

Raistrick, A. (with Chapman, S.E.) (1929), The Lynchet Groups of Upper Wharfdale, *Antiquity* iii, 165–181.

Raistrick, A. (1937), Prehistoric cultivation at Grassington, *Yorkshire Archaeol.* xxxiii, 166–174.

Raistrick, A. (1939), Iron Age Settlements in West Yorkshire, *Yorkshire Archaeol.* xxxiv, 115–150.

Renfrew, J.M. (1973), *Palaeoethnobotany* (London).

Richardson, G.G.S. (1973), The Roman Tilery, Scalesceugh, CW_2, lxxiii 79.

Richardson, G.G.S. (1977), A Romano-British Farmstead at Fingland, Cumberland, CW_2 lxxvii.

Richmond, I.A. (1933), Castle Folds, by Great Ashby, CW_2 xxxiii, 233–237.

Richmond, I.A. (1951), A Roman Arterial Signalling System in the Stainmore Pass, in W.F. Grimes (Ed.) *Aspects in Archaeology in Britain and Beyond*, (London) 293–303.

Richmond, I.A. (1969), *Roman Archaeology and Art* (London).

Richmond, I.A. and Crawford, O.G.S. (1949), The British Section of the Ravenna Cosmography, *Archaeologia*, xciii, 1.

Richmond, I.A. and Gillam, J.P. (1952), The Solway House Milecastles, CW_2 lii, 17.

Ritchie, A. (1970), Palisaded sites in Northern Britain: their context and affinities, *Scottish Archaeol. Forum*, ii, 48–67.

Rivet, A.L.F. and Smith, C. (1979), *The Place Names of Roman Britain* (London).

Rollinson, W. (1967), *A History of Man in the Lake District* (London).

Ross, A. (1961), The Horned God of the Brigantes, *Archaeologia Aeliana* 4, xxxix, 63.

Ross, A. (1967), *Pagan Celtic Britain* (London).

Ross, P. (1920), The Roman road north of Low Borrowbridge to Brougham Castle, *CW₂* xx, 1–15.

Royal Commission on the Ancient Monuments and Constructions of England (1936) *An inventory of the historical monuments of Westmorland* (London).

Salway, P. (1965) *The Frontier People of Roman Britain* (Cambridge).

Simpson, W.D. (1959), Brocavum, Ninkirk and Brougham: a study in continuity, *CW₂* lviii, 68–87.

Shaw, R.C. (1964), *Post-Roman Carlisle and the Kingdoms of the North-West* (Preston).

Shotter, D.C.A. (1979), The evidence of coin-loss and the Roman occupation of Northwest England, in N.J. Higham (Ed.) *The Changing Past* (Manchester).

Smith, C.A. (1977), Late Prehistoric and Romano-British Homesteads in N.W. Wales: an interpretation of their Morphology, *Archaeologia Cambrensis* xxxviii, 126.

Spence, J.E. (1933), Preliminary Report on the Petteril Green Camp, *CW₂* xxxiii, 227–232.

Stevens, C.E. (1937), Gildas and the Lost Cities of Britain, *English Hist. Rev.* lii, 193.

Stevens, C.E. (1951), A Roman Author in Northwest Britain, *CW₂* 1, 70.

Stevens, C.E. (1966), The Social and economic aspects of rural settlement, in C. Thomas (Ed.) *Rural Settlement in Roman Britain* (London) 108–128.

Stukeley, W. (1776), *Itinerarium Curiosum II* (London).

Thomas, A.C. (1966) (Ed.), *Rural Settlement in Roman Britain* (London).

Thomas, A.C. (1971), *The Early Christian Archaeology of North Britain* (Oxford).

Thomas, A.C. (1974), *Britain and Ireland in Early Christian Times* (Swindon).

Thomas, A.C. (1981), *Christianity in Roman Britain to AD 500* (London).

Tierney, J.J. (1959–60), The Celtic Ethnography of Posidonius, *Proc. Royal Irish Acad.* lx, 189–275.

Victoria County History (1901–05) *Cumberland*, Ed. J. Wilson (London).

Wacher, J. (1975), *The Towns of Roman Britain* (London).

Walker, D. (1965), Excavations at Barnscar, *CW₂* lxv, 53–65.

Ware, Rev. C. (1883), A British Rath near Kirkby Lonsdale, *CW₁* vii, 111–113.

Webster, P.V. (1972), Severn Valley Ware on Hadrian's Wall, *Archaeologia Aeliana* 4, 1, 191.

Webster, P.V. (1979), Romano-British Coarse Pottery in the North-West, in N.J. Higham (Ed.) *The Changing Past* (Manchester) 15ff.

Webster, R.A. (1969), *The Romano-British settlements in Westmorland — a study in cultural ecology*. (Unpublished PhD Thesis, Reading University).

Webster, R.A. (1971), A morphological study of Romano-British settlements in Westmorland, CW_2 lxxi, 64–71.

Webster, R.A. (1972), The excavation of a Romano-British settlement at Waitby, CW_2 lxxii, 66–73.

Wheeler, R.E.M. (1954), *The Stanwick Fortifications* (Oxford).

Whellan, T. (1860), *History and Antiquities of Cumberland and Westmorland* (London).

Williams, I. (1951), Wales and the North, CW_2 li, 73–88.

Wilson, P.A. (1978), Eaglesfield: the plce, the name, the burials, CW_2, LXXVIII, 47–54.

Wright, R.P. and Philips, E.J. (1975), *Roman Inscribed and Sculptured Stones in Carlisle Museum* (Carlisle).

Index